101
PEOPLE WHO CHANGED THE WORLD

An imprint of Om Books International

First published in 2019 by

Om KIDZ | Om Books International

Corporate & Editorial Office
A-12, Sector 64, Noida 201 301
Uttar Pradesh, India
Phone: +91 120 477 4100
Email: editorial@ombooks.com
Website: www.ombooksinternational.com

Sales Office
107, Ansari Road, Darya Ganj
New Delhi 110 002, India
Phone: +91 11 4000 9000
Email: sales@ombooks.com
Website: www.ombooks.com

© Om Books International 2019

ALL RIGHTS RESERVED. No part of this book may be reproduced or transmitted in any form by any means, electronic or mechanical, including photocopying and recording, or by any information storage and retrieval system, except as may be expressly permitted in writing by the publisher.

ISBN: 978-93-86316-11-0

Printed in India

10 9 8 7 6 5 4 3 2 1

101
PEOPLE WHO CHANGED THE WORLD

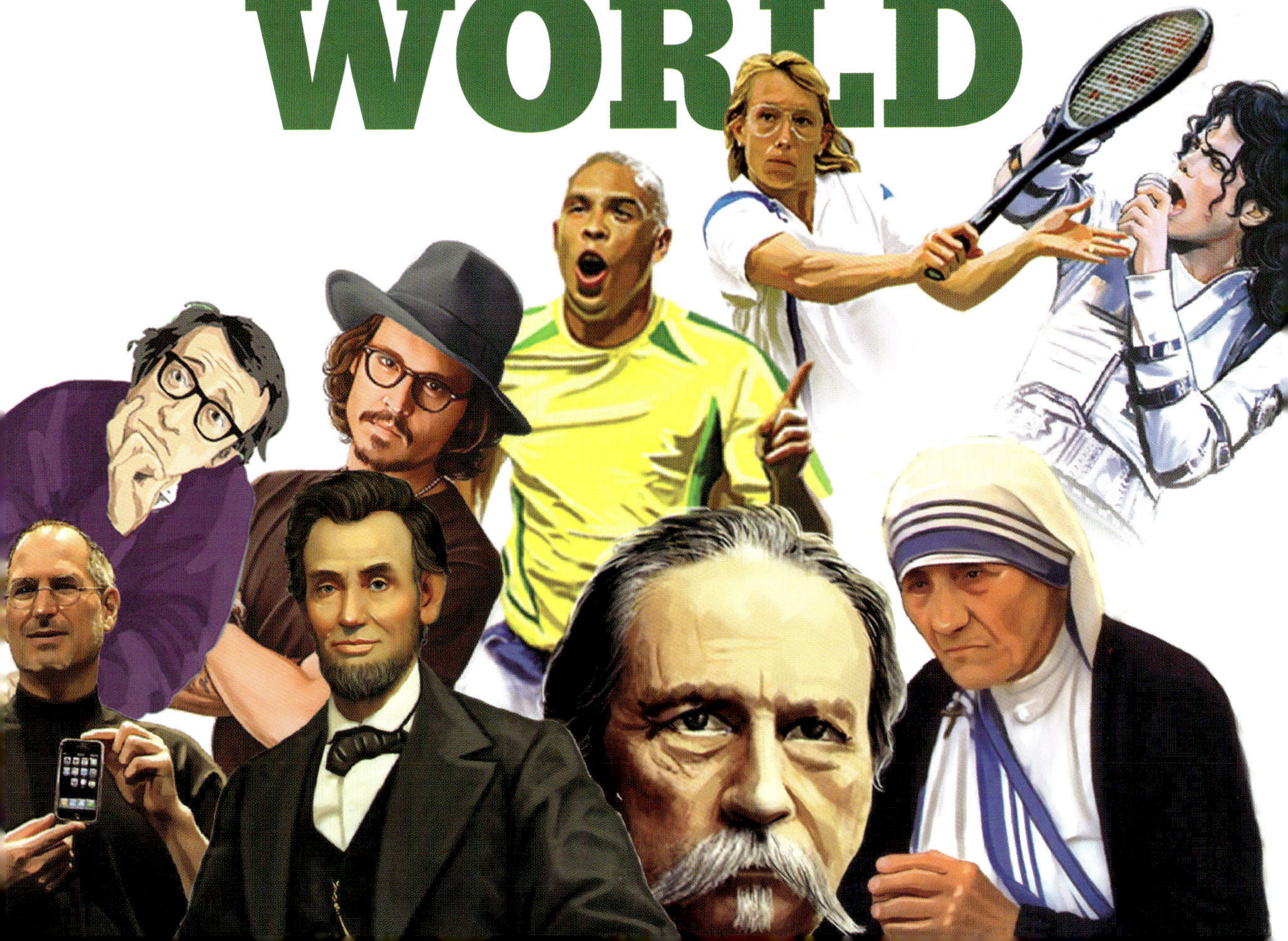

Contents

Amazing Artists

01. Leonardo Da Vinci — 10
02. Claude Monet — 11
03. Vincent Van Gogh — 12
04. Edvard Munch — 13
05. Pablo Picasso — 14
06. Ansel Adams — 15
07. Salvador Dali — 16
08. Jackson Pollock — 17
09. Andy Warhol — 18

Business Boomers

10. Henry Ford — 20
11. Warren Buffett — 20
12. JRD Tata — 22
13. Bill Gates — 22
14. Steve Jobs — 24
15. Steve Wozniak — 25
16. Jeff Bezos — 26
17. Larry Page and Sergey Brin — 27
18. Mark Zuckerberg — 28

Fabulous Fashionistas

19. Charles Lewis Tiffany — 30
20. Coco Chanel — 31
21. Mario Prada — 32
22. Giorgio Armani — 33
23. Donna Karan — 34

Greater Good

24. Helen Keller — 36
25. Mother Teresa — 37
26. Florence Nightingale — 38
27. Oprah Winfrey — 39
28. Princess Diana — 40

Incredible Innovators

29. Nicolaus Copernicus — 42
30. Galileo Galilei — 43
31. Isaac Newton — 44
32. Benjamin Franklin — 45
33. James Watt — 46
34. Charles Babbage — 47
35. Louis Braille — 48
36. Charles Darwin — 49
37. Thomas Edison — 50
38. Alexander Graham Bell — 51
39. Nikola Tesla — 52
40. The Wright Brothers — 53
41. Guglielmo Marconi — 54
42. Albert Einstein — 55
43. Alexander Fleming — 56
44. Stephen hawking — 58

Legendary Leaders

45. Alexander the Great — 60
46. Julius Caesar — 61
47. Constantine — 62
48. Joan of Arc — 63
49. Lorenzo de' Medici — 64
50. Henry VIII — 65
51. Queen Elizabeth I — 66
52. Thomas Jefferson — 67
53. Abraham Lincoln — 68
54. Theodore Roosevelt — 69

55.	Mahatma Gandhi	70
56.	Winston Churchill	71
57.	John F. Kennedy	72
58.	Margaret Thatcher	73
59.	Indira Gandhi	74
60.	Martin Luther King Jr.	75
61.	Benazir Bhutto	76

Lights, Camera, Action!

62.	Charlie Chaplin	77
63.	Walt Disney	78
64.	Warner Brothers	79
65.	Steven Spielberg	79
66.	Tim Burton	80

Literary Lords

67.	Dante Alighieri	85
68.	William Shakespeare	86
69.	Jane Austen	87
70.	Lewis Carroll	88
71.	Arthur Conan Doyle	90
72.	Oscar Wilde	91
73.	Rabindranath Tagore	92
74.	William Randolph Hearst	93
75.	William Butler Yeats	94
76.	J.R.R.Tolkien	95
77.	F.Scott Fitzgerald	96
78.	Enid Blyton	97
79.	J.K.Rowling	98

Mesmerising Musicians

80.	Beethoven	100
81.	Miles Dewey Davis	101
82.	Elvis Presley	102
83.	John Lennon	103
84.	Bob Dylan	104
85.	Bob Marley	105
86.	David Bowie	106
87.	Madonna	107
88.	Michael Jackson	108
89.	The Beatles	109
90.	ABBA	110

Phenomenal Philoshophers

91.	Socrates	112
92.	Aristotle	113
93.	Plato	114
94.	Sigmund Freud	116
95.	Noam Chomsky	118

Sports Stars

96.	Muhammad Ali	120
97.	Steffi Graf	121
98.	Ronaldo	122
99.	Roger Federer	123
100.	The Williams Sisters	124
101.	Usain Bolt	126

Amazing Artists

This section focuses on people who have laid the stepping stone in the field of art. Their work has contributed to shaping the art world in a major way. Let's find out about their masterpieces and contributions as well as their lives. Read on and get to know these amazing artists.

01. LEONARDO DA VINCI

Leonardo da Vinci was an artist, scientist and inventor during the Italian Renaissance. He was born on 15 April 1452 in Vinci, Italy. He is hailed as one of the most talented and intelligent people of all time.

Not much is known about his childhood, except for the fact that his father was a rich man. He worked as an apprentice with a famous artist named Verrocchio when he was 14 years old. He learned all about art, drawing, painting and more.

Da Vinci kept journals where he would draw and write about his scientific observations of the world. His journals were filled with diagrams of hand gliders, helicopters, war machines, musical instruments, various pumps and anything else that caught his fancy.

Da Vinci is regarded as one of the greatest artists in history. He created several masterpieces throughout his lifetime, the most well-known of which are *The Last Supper* and *The Mona Lisa*. He died on 2 May 1519.

02. CLAUDE MONET

Claude Monet was a French painter who founded the Impressionist Movement. He was born on 14 November 1840, in Paris. He enjoyed drawing ever since he was a child. He started by drawing very impressive caricatures of people.

He scribbled caricatures of his teachers in his schoolbooks and by 15, had gained a reputation as a caricature artist. His work was displayed at a local frame maker's shop. People soon began recognising their friends and acquaintances in the drawings. It was not long before he started charging people to draw their caricatures and this gave him a steady income.

Monet became known as an *'Impressionist'*—a title derived from his painting, *Impression, Sunrise.* The brush strokes were lively and spontaneous, capturing the feeling of the moment.

Monet was one of the first artists to paint outdoors. Though paintings of landscapes were common, they were almost always painted from recollection in a studio and never a direct impression. Monet died on 5 December 1926.

IMPORTANT FACT
Impressionism was a form of art characterised by small, thin, yet visible strokes. Impressionists believed in capturing the essence of the subject instead of the detail.

03. VINCENT VAN GOGH

Vincent Van Gogh was a Dutch painter, who is one of the greatest post-impressionist painters. He was born on 30 March 1853 in Netherlands.

His work was a major influence on 20th century art. He struggled with psychological illnesses and was poor throughout his life. He was also virtually unrecognised throughout his life.

At 16, he apprenticed with a branch of art dealers. Dealing with art on a daily basis aroused an artistic sensibility in him and he soon began to admire Dutch masters like Rembrandt. He later tried his hand at many professions, including teaching, and he even tried joining the Church. However, he was thrown out of the church and took to painting after that.

His paintings became popular only after his death. They were characterised by bright colours, deliberate brush strokes and forced forms. His painting, *The Starry Night*, has become one of the most celebrated art masterpieces of all time.

Van Gogh pioneered the art movement that came to be known as '*Expressionism*'. He died in France on 29 July 1890 from a self-inflicted gunshot wound.

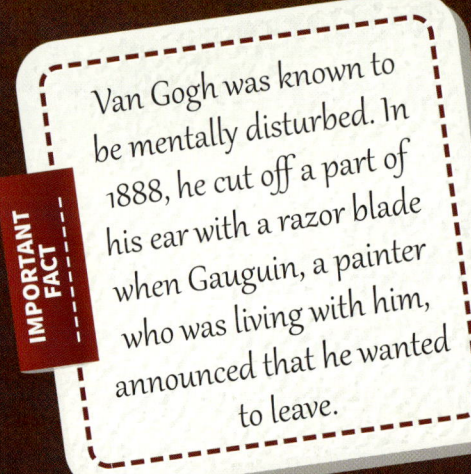

IMPORTANT FACT

Van Gogh was known to be mentally disturbed. In 1888, he cut off a part of his ear with a razor blade when Gauguin, a painter who was living with him, announced that he wanted to leave.

04. EDVARD MUNCH

IMPORTANT FACT

Post stamp printed in Norge shows *The Sick Child* painting

Edvard Munch, a Norwegian painter, greatly influenced German expressionism. He was born on 12 December 1863 in Löten, Norway. He began to pursue a career in engineering, but abandoned it and decided to devote his life to painting. He established a style of painting that was free flowing. His paintings reflected his internal emotions and was like nothing anyone had ever seen before. His painting, '*The Scream*' is possibly one of the most recognisable works in the history of art. His later works were not as intense as his earlier ones, but his legacy was already established. He died on 23 January 1944.

THE ORIGINAL PAINTING

THE SICK CHILD BY EDVARD MUNCH

05. PABLO PICASSO

Pablo Picasso was one of the greatest artists of the 20th century and also one of the pioneers of the Cubism art form. He was born on 25 October 1881 in Malaga, Spain. His father was an art teacher and this helped cultivate Picasso's interest. His father began tutoring him in art from the age of seven. Picasso kept practising until he was an even better artist than his father.

At the age of 16, Picasso started attending Madrid's Royal Academy of San Fernando. When he went to Paris in 1900, Picasso's art attracted the attention of several art collectors, including the famous Gertrude Stein. 1907 marked the year that Picasso created Les Demoiselles d'Avignon, which laid the foundation for the Cubism art movement. Cubism involves breaking up the painting's subject and re-assembling it on the canvas in an abstract composition.

IMPORTANT FACT: Pablo Picasso's full name has 22 words! He was baptised as Pablo Diego José Francisco de Paula Juan Nepomuceno María de los Remedios Cipriano de la Santísima Trinidad Martyr Patricio Clito Ruíz y Picasso. He was named after several saints and relatives.

Some of his famous paintings include *The Old Guitarist*, *Asleep* and *Seated Woman* and *Guernica*, a mural about the Spanish Civil War. Pablo Picasso died on 8 April 1973 in Mougins, France.

06. ANSEL ADAMS

Ansel Adams, a famous American photographer and environmentalist, was born on 20 February 1902. He is one of America's most loved photographers. He was known to work exhausting hours, sometimes more than 18 hours a day. He learned from and exhibited with other famous photographers of the time. Most of his important works were photographs of America's wilderness. He died in Monterey, California, on 22 April 1984.

HIS ICONIC BLACK-AND-WHITE IMAGES HELPED TO ESTABLISH PHOTOGRAPHY AMONG THE FINE ARTS.

07. SALVADOR DALI

THE PERSISTENCE OF MEMORY IS A 1931 PAINTING BY ARTIST SALVADOR DALI, AND IS ONE OF HIS MOST RECOGNISABLE WORKS.

ORIGINAL PAINTING

Salvador Dali, a Spanish surrealist painter and printmaker, was born on 11 May 1904 in Figueres, Spain. He was adept at several styles. However, two events greatly influenced his style. He read Freud's work on dreams and the subconscious. He also met a group of Paris surrealists. The surreal movement in art and literature believed in the power of man's subconscious over reality. He often presented everyday objects in a dreamlike absurd manner. Today, he is one of the best known surrealists of all times. He died on 23 January 1989.

08. JACKSON POLLOCK

Paul Jackson Pollock, an American painter known for his involvement in the Abstract Expressionist Movement, was born on 28 January 1912. He gained fame during his lifetime itself. He was first exposed to liquid paint at a workshop in New York City held by Mexican muralist, David Alfaro Siqueiros in 1936. Later, paint pouring was one of several techniques he used on canvases in the early 1940s. Some of his famous works include *Male and Female* and *Composition with Pouring I*. He died on 11 August 1956.

MOVIE POSTER

POLLOCK WAS THE SUBJECT OF THE OSCAR-WINNING FILM 'POLLOCK' DIRECTED BY AND STARRING ED HARRIS.

09. ANDY WARHOL

Andy Warhol is an American artist and filmmaker. He was born on 6 August 1928. He was an initiator of the Pop Art movement, which propagated the mass production of art and swept the USA in the 1960s. He studied fine art in college, after which he moved to New York City and began creating advertisements and illustrations for magazines. Warhol began creating the paintings he is best known for today in the 1960s. He loved pop culture and decided to paint what he loved. He painted large pictures of Coca-Cola bottles, Campbell's soup cans and dollar bills. He also painted pictures of celebrities. He died on 22 February 1987.

POP ART

AFTER HER SUDDEN DEATH FROM AN OVERDOSE OF SLEEPING PILLS IN AUGUST 1962, SUPERSTAR MARILYN MONROE'S LIFE, CAREER AND TRAGEDY BECAME A WORLDWIDE OBSESSION. WARHOL, BEING INFATUATED WITH FAME AND POP CULTURE, OBTAINED A BLACK-AND-WHITE PUBLICITY PHOTO OF HER (FROM HER 1953 FILM NIAGARA) AND USED THE PHOTO TO CREATE SEVERAL SERIES OF IMAGES.

Business Boomers

This section focuses on people who have become super successful by revolutionising businesses. Their work has contributed to providing opportunities to the world, too. Let's learn not only about their success stories, but also their personal lives. Read on and get to know these business boomers.

10. HENRY FORD

FORD QUADRICYCLE

AN 1896 FORD, A GASOLINE-POWERED MOTOR CAR WHICH ITS MAKER HENRY FORD CALLED 'QUADRICYCLE.'

Henry Ford, an American industrialist, founded the Ford Motor Company. He was born on 30 July 1863 in Michigan, USA. At the age of 19, Ford made a tractor from an old mowing machine and a steam engine. Later, he developed a gasoline-powered vehicle known as the Ford Quadricycle in 1896. It was a vehicle mounted on four bicycle wheels and looked like a horseless carriage. He then met Thomas Edison who encouraged him to develop a better second model. 'Model T' was launched in 1908 and became an instant success. Ford also developed a system of assembly line production that led to the mass production of cars. He passed away on 7 April 1947.

11. WARREN BUFFETT

Warren Buffett is an American investor and business tycoon believed to be one of the most successful investors of the 20th century. He was born on 30 August 1930 in Nebraska, USA. Even as a child, Buffett enjoyed investing, earning and saving money. Buffett bought three shares of a company at the young age of 11.

Buffett graduated with a degree in Business Administration from the University of Nebraska, Lincoln. Buffett, at age 20, had earned almost $10,000 from his childhood businesses. He joined the Columbia Business School and earned a Masters degree in 1951. He formed his firm, Buffett Partnership in his hometown Omaha. Buffett invested in undervalued companies whose stocks shortly began to rise. This made him extremely rich and gained him the title—'Oracle of Omaha'. In 1965, Buffett became a majority holder in the textile firm, Berkshire Hathaway Inc., the success of which made him one of the wealthiest men in America.

IMPORTANT FACT

In 2006, Buffett announced that he would give away 99% of his fortune to charity (about $62 billion), mainly to the Bill and Melinda Gates Foundation. Warren Buffett was awarded the Presidential Medal of Freedom in 2011.

12. JRD TATA

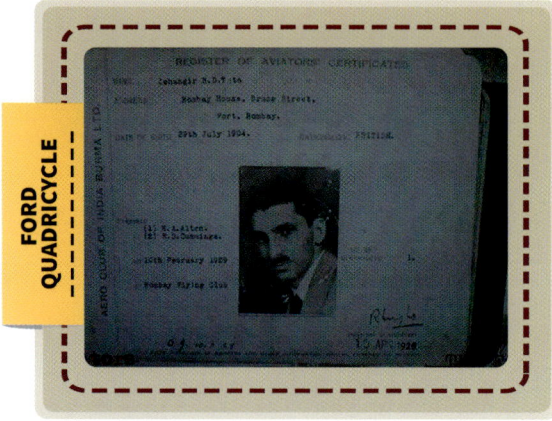

JRD TATA –
THE FIRST LICENCED
PILOT IN INDIA

JRD Tata was an Indian businessman who pioneered India's first airline and laid the foundation of Tata Group, India's largest industrial empire. He was born on 29 July 1904 in Paris, France. JRD went to different schools in Paris, Mumbai and Yokohama.

JRD founded Tata Motors in 1945. He was the first licenced pilot in India and launched India's first international airline. He was the director of the Tata Group of companies that excelled in the field of technology, hospitality, chemicals, power, engineering and automobiles. He died on 29 November 1993.

13. BILL GATES

William Henry Gates III, better known as Bill Gates, is an American programmer, inventor and entrepreneur. He was born on 28 October 1955 in Seattle, Washington, USA. Bill Gates wrote his first computer software programme at the age of 13.

Gates left Harvard to devote his career to Microsoft, a company he started in 1975 with his old friend Paul Allen. He started by developing software for micro-computers. Microsoft licenced an operating system named MS-DOS for use on IBM PC, i.e. personal computer. Gradually, all companies wanted Microsoft software and Microsoft went on to become the world's largest personal computer software company. Gates is not only a tech guru, he is also a popular writer! *The Road Ahead*, his book, was published in 1995. He also wrote *Business @ the Speed of Thought* in 1999, a book that shows how computer technology can solve business problems in new ways.

IMPORTANT FACT

Bill Gates is believed to be one of the richest people in the world. In addition to his work, he is also famous for his charitable organisation, the Bill and Melinda Gates Foundation. It funds health programmes, provides study grants and many other programmes on global development.

14. STEVE JOBS

Steven Paul Jobs was an American inventor and entrepreneur who co-founded Apple Inc. He was born on 24 February 1955 in California, USA. He was adopted at birth by Paul and Clara Jobs. The family moved from San Francisco to Mountain View, a suburban town in Santa Clara county, also known as Silicon Valley.

Jobs was introduced to Steve Wozniak by a mutual friend in 1970 with whom he shared a common love of electronics. Together, they created the Apple I and Apple II computers. While Jobs concentrated on the design, Wozniak took responsibility of the electronics. The Apple II was the first personal computer capable of colour graphics. Jobs insisted that Apple should design all the software and hardware of all Apple products. Jobs started 'Pixar Animation Studios' after he bought the computer graphics division of 'Lucasfilm' in 1986. Jobs has been described as a perfectionist, brilliant, self-centred and temperamental person. Not only was he a businessman and a technologist, he was also an artist and a designer. He passed away on 5 October 2011.

IMPORTANT FACT

JOBS WAS CREDITED AS THE EXECUTIVE PRODUCER OF THE ANIMATED MOVIE, TOY STORY.

15. STEVE WOZNIAK

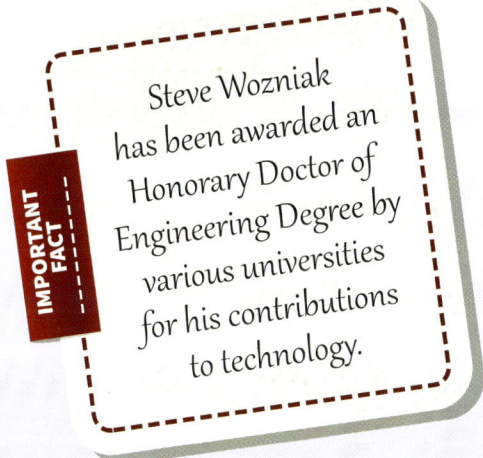

IMPORTANT FACT

Steve Wozniak has been awarded an Honorary Doctor of Engineering Degree by various universities for his contributions to technology.

Steve Wozniak, an American computer engineer and programmer, co-founded the company Apple Inc. in partnership with his friend, Steve Jobs. He was born on 11 August 1950 in California, USA. He was fascinated by electronics at an early age. Steve Wozniak met Steve Jobs through a mutual friend during his brief stint at the University of California in Berkeley. Wozniak quit his job at Hewlett-Packard to team up with Steve Jobs and formed Apple Computers in 1976.

Wozniak only enjoyed engineering and not management. As many other engineers joined Apple, Wozniak no longer felt needed there. He ended his full-time employment with Apple permanently on 6 February 1985, 12 years after having founded the company. Wozniak founded a new venture called CL 9, which developed and brought the first programmable universal remote control to market in 1987. In 2002, Wozniak founded Wheels of Zeus (WOZ) to create wireless GPS technology. Wozniak published his autobiography, *iWoz: From Computer Geek to Cult Icon: How I Invented the Personal Computer, Co-Founded Apple, and Had Fun Doing It*.

16. JEFF BEZOS

WHEN THE AMAZON.COM FIRST WENT LIVE, IT ONLY SOLD BOOKS. THE FIRST BOOK SOLD WAS FLUID CONCEPTS AND CREATIVE ANALOGIES BY DOUGLAS HOFSTADTE.

Jeff Bezos, an American entrepreneur and investor is famous as the e-commerce pioneer who started Amazon.com, Inc. He was born on 12 January 1964 in New Mexico, USA. Bezos studied electrical engineering and computer science at Princeton University.

Bezos quit his lucrative job at an investment bank to open a virtual bookstore called 'Amazon.com'. Amazon.com became the leader of e-commerce and one of Internet's biggest success stories. Bezos purchased *The Washington Post* in a $250 million deal in 2013. This business boomer has broadened his market with Amazon offering the sale of videos, CDs, clothes, electronics, toys, jewellery and beauty products throughout the world.

17. LARRY PAGE AND SERGEY BRIN

Larry Page and Sergey Brin are computer scientists who co-founded Google, the online search engine. Larry Page was born on 26 March 1973 and Sergey Brin was born on 21 August 1973 in Moscow. Brin's family migrated to the USA to escape Jewish persecution in 1979, where he met Page at Stanford University.

They developed a new search engine technology which they named 'Google', based on the mathematical term 'googol' which means 1 followed by 100 zeros. After its launch in 1998, Google has become the most popular search engine in the world.

IMPORTANT FACT

10,000,000,000,000,000,000,000,000,000,000,000,000,000,000,000,000,000,000,000,000,000,000,000,000,000,000,000,000,000,000,000,000,000,000,000,000,000,000,000 is equal to 1 googol

THE NAME 'GOOGLE' IS ACTUALLY DERIVED FROM THE MATHEMATICAL TERM 'GOOGOL' WHICH IS BASICALLY 1 WITH A 100 ZEROS FOLLOWING IT

18. MARK ZUCKERBERG

Mark Elliot Zuckerberg is an American computer programmer and entrepreneur who co-founded Facebook, a social networking website. He was born on 14 May 1984 in New York, USA. Zuckerberg studied at the Phillips Exeter Academy. He used computers and started writing computer programmes in middle school. Later, he joined Harvard University in 2002.

While he was at Harvard, along with his roommates, he started a social website called thefacebook.com, where Harvard students could put in their personal details in a template he had developed. The website developed by Zuckerberg was different as it laid emphasis on real email addresses and names. He was helped by his roommates Dustin Moskovitz and Chris Hughes. Zuckerberg left Harvard to work on his new company, Facebook. He launched Facebook in 2004 and by 2006, anyone with an email address could join Facebook. Facebook has more than 1.19 billion users now, making Zuckerberg a billionaire. The story of the birth of Facebook was depicted in the film, *The Social Network*.

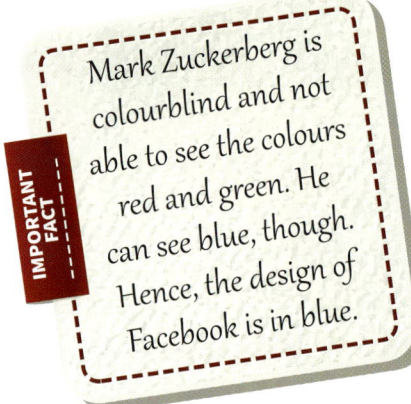

IMPORTANT FACT: Mark Zuckerberg is colourblind and not able to see the colours red and green. He can see blue, though. Hence, the design of Facebook is in blue.

Fabulous Fashionistas

This section focuses on people who have laid out the concepts for modern clothing. Their work has majorly contributed to the fashion industry. Let us find out about their inventions and developments as well as about their lives. Read on and get to know these fashionable stalwarts.

19. CHARLES LEWIS TIFFANY

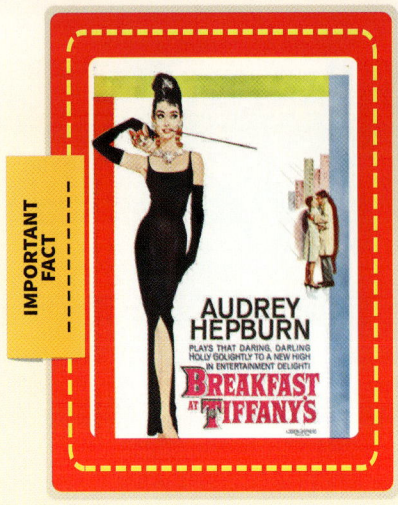

THE ICONIC MOVIE, 'BREAKFAST AT TIFFANY'S' MARKED THE FIRST TIME FILMING WAS ALLOWED INSIDE THE STORE.

Charles Tiffany, the founder of American jewellery chain 'Tiffany & Co.', was born on 15 February 1812 in Connecticut, USA. In 1837, along with his school friend John Young, he started a shop named 'Tiffany & Young'. At the time, they sold stationery and gift items. Slowly, they ventured into glassware, cutlery, clocks and jewellery.

A third partner entered in 1841 and the shop's offering evolved. They sold only the finest, top-quality products. They also began making their own jewellery. Tiffany bought his partners' shares in the shop in 1853 and renamed it 'Tiffany & Co.'

By 1868, Tiffany had four stores in locations including London and Paris. This has now increased to over 200. He is also credited with inventing the retail catalogue which allows customers to view and select designs from a brochure. He died on 18 February 1902.

20. COCO CHANEL

IMPORTANT FACT

COCO CHANEL STARTED HER FASHION CAREER BY DESIGNING HATS. WITH THE HELP OF ONE OF HER MALE ADMIRERS, SHE OPENED HER FIRST SHOP IN PARIS IN 1913. AS IT BECAME MORE POPULAR, SHE STARTED SELLING CLOTHES AS WELL.

French fashion designer Coco Chanel is one of the biggest fashion icons of all time. She was born as Gabrielle Bonheur Chanel on 19 August 1883 in Saumur, France. After the death of her mother, Chanel was sent to an orphanage where she learnt how to sew. She got the nickname 'Coco' during her short-lived career as a cabaret singer. Chanel picked up hat-making and opened her own hat shop in 1910. By the 1920s, she had already launched her signature perfume 'Chanel No. 5' and 'Little Black Dress'. She died on 10 January 1971 in Paris.

21. MARIO PRADA

Mario Prada was the founder and original designer of the Italian fashion label 'Prada', a label that creates high-fashion goods for men and women. He started the label with his brother, Martino Prada as a leather goods shop in 1913.

Mario felt that women should not have a role in the business world. He prevented female members of his family from entering his company. However, Mario's son did not want to work for the label, so his daughter Luisia Prada took over from Mario and ran the business for almost 20 years.

Prada started its business by making bags and suitcases. These were a huge success, which led to the designing and launch of the first ready-to-wear Prada collection. Its clean lines, classic colours and luxury fabrics made it a huge success.

Prada was known for being ahead of its time during the 1990s. It had an ultramodern industrial sleekness which placed it apart from the other fashion brands of the time. Mario Prada died in 1958.

IMPORTANT FACT

Mario did not want his company to be run by the women in his family. But his son had no interest in the family business, so it was taken over by his daughter and, later, his granddaughter. Mario's granddaughter Miuccia, took over the family business from her mother in 1978, when the company was going through a financial struggle.

22. GIORGIO ARMANI

IMPORTANT FACT

Armani had planned to become a doctor. He was always fascinated by the human body and even went to medical school at the University of Milan. However, he stopped studying and joined the army.

Born on 11 July 1934 in Italy, Giorgio Armani is an iconic fashion designer, primarily known for the 'power suits' that he designed for men.

By working as a salesperson at a Milan department store, Armani gained experience about the fashion industry and its working. He then became a designer for menswear at the Nino Cerruti company. He quickly soared to popularity and, by 1975, he had launched his own fashion label.

Armani went on to introduce many new lines like the Armani Jeans and Armani Junior. But the most revolutionary line was the Emporio Armani line, which made his stylish designs accessible at lower prices.

In order to publicise his Emporio Armani line, he resorted to unconventional advertising methods like designing clothes for TV shows and films. He was also the first designer to promote a healthy body image among his models by refusing to employ people with a lower than healthy BMI. In 2007, he teamed up with Samsung to design the Giorgio Armani phone.

23. DONNA KARAN

Donna Karan is an American designer known for the simple, comfortable design of her clothes. She was born on 2 October 1948. Her father was a tailor and her mother, a model. She attended Parsons School of Design but dropped out in 1968 and started working for sportswear designer, Anne Klein. In 1984, she launched her own line, the Donna Karan Co., which eventually became DKNY. In 2004, she received a Lifetime Achievement Award from the Council of Fashion Designers of America.

Greater Good

This section focuses on people who have worked for the betterment of society even if it meant sacrificing their freedom. Let's find out about their contributions and charities as well as about their lives. Read on and get to know these Miracle Workers.

24. HELEN KELLER

Helen Adams Keller was an American author, political activist and lecturer, who was famous for being the first deaf–blind person to earn a Bachelor of Arts degree. Keller was born on 27 June 1880 in Alabama, USA. She became blind and deaf when she was eighteen months old. Her teacher Anne Sullivan played a very important role in her life.

Keller participated in many campaigns to raise awareness, money and support for the blind. She was appointed Councillor of International Relations for the American Foundation of Overseas Blind. She died on 1 June 1968.

25. MOTHER TERESA

Mother Teresa or 'Blessed Mother Teresa of Kolkata' as she is popularly known, was a world famous humanitarian. She was born on 26 August 1910 in Skopje, Republic of Macedonia. Her birth name was Agnes Gonxha Bojaxhiu. It is believed that Agnes loved the stories of the missionaries of Bengal. At the age of 12, she decided to commit her life to religion.

Agnes joined the Sisters of Loretto in Ireland in 1928. She then taught in an Order's school in Kolkata for 17 years. In 1946, she believed that she experienced a divine intervention that she was to devote her life to helping the poor and needy. Mother Teresa learnt basic medical training at Holy Family Hospital Patna and started helping poor people, especially in the slums of Kolkata. Mother Teresa founded the Missionaries of Charity, a religious congregation aimed to care for the poor, ill and homeless people. She extended care to lepers and cripples who were unloved and shunned by society. She died on 5 September 1997.

26. FLORENCE NIGHTINGALE

Florence Nightingale, often called the 'Lady with the Lamp', was a social reformer, statistician and the founder of modern nursing. She was born on 12 May 1820 in Florence, Italy. She assisted the ill and the poor from a very young age. She believed that nursing was her divine purpose. Nightingale nursed the British and the allied soldiers during the Crimean War. She established the St. Thomas Hospital and the Nightingale Training School for Nurses in 1860 to formalise nursing. She turned hospitals into cleaner spaces and proved that trained nurses and clean hospitals helped sick people get better. She often walked around the wards at night carrying a lantern in her hand, which is why she came to be known as the 'Lady with the Lamp'. She died on 13 August 1910.

IMPORTANT FACT

Florence Nightingale's maths skills were as excellent as her nursing skills. She used statistics to better understand health care.

27. OPRAH WINFREY

Oprah Winfrey is an actress, philanthropist and one of the most popular television anchors who is famous for her talk show—The Oprah Winfrey Show. She was born on 29 January 1954 in Kosciusko, USA. Winfrey graduated from Tenesse State University and secured a job as a co-anchor and reporter for ABC News in Baltimore.

Winfrey hosted a talk show, 'AM Chicago' by a Chicago TV station, which became very popular. She then started her own talk show, 'The Oprah Winfrey Show', which made her one of the most popular and richest people in the USA. The Oprah Winfrey Show was aired for almost two and a half decades.

Winfrey is listed as the world's richest woman of the 20th century by the Forbes magazine. She has also been hailed as the most influential woman of her generation. She founded Oprah's Angel Network that supports many charitable organisations.

IMPORTANT FACT

Winfrey has co-authored five books and runs a magazine named O, the Oprah Magazine. She has also lent her name to animated films like Charlotte's Web and Princess and the Frog.

28. PRINCESS DIANA

Diana, Princess of Wales, was the first wife of Prince Charles, the heir apparent to Queen Elizabeth II. She was born as Diana Spencer on 1 July 1961. Although she was not good at academics, she was an accomplished pianist. Diana married Prince Charles on 29 July 1981. She was one of the most loved and adored members of the British royal family.

Princess Diana used her international celebrity status to help raise awareness about illnesses, poverty, drug abuse and homelessness. She upheld the cause of AIDS, child abuse and leprosy. Princess Diana founded as well as associated herself with many charities. Even after her divorce from Prince Charles in 1996, she continued to work for different charitable organisations. Princess Diana was deeply involved in efforts to ban land mines.

Her popularity as a member of the Royal family brought unprecedented attention to her public and private life. She became one of the most photographed personalities in the world.

Diana was killed in a car accident while trying to evade journalists on 31 August 1997 in Paris, France.

Incredible Innovators

This section focuses on innovators whose work has contributed to important innovations. Let's find out about their inventions and contributions as well as their lives. Read on and get to know these incredible innovators better.

29. NICOLAUS COPERNICUS

Nicolaus Copernicus was a Polish mathematician, scholar, economist, artist, diplomat and an astronomer. He was born on 19 February 1473 in Torun, Poland. In 1496, he travelled to Italy to study law. Copernicus is best known for his theory '*De Revolutionibus Orbium Coelestium*', meaning 'On the Revolutions of the Celestial Spheres'.

Copernicus' theory was commonly known as 'heliocentrism'. It states that the sun is at the centre of the universe, while earth and all the other planets rotate around it in circular paths. It was Copernicus' theory that led to an astronomical revolution. His theory greatly influenced many great scientists including Galileo, Kepler, Descartes and Newton.

Copernicus came up with this theory between 1508 and 1514. He wrote this in a manuscript called the *Commentariolus* (Little Commentary). However, the final version of his theory was published in 1543, the year he died. He passed away on 24 May 1543.

IMPORTANT FACT: We know certain facts about Copernicus' early life. But a biography written by his ardent disciple, Georg Joachim Rheticus, is unfortunately lost.

30. GALILEO GALILEI

Galileo Galilei was an Italian mathematician, astronomer, physicist and philosopher. He was born on 15 February 1564 in Pisa, Italy. He grew up during the Italian Renaissance, which greatly influenced him. Galileo began his education at the Camaldolese monastery. He was an accomplished musician and an excellent student. He went to the University of Pisa to study medicine in 1581, but soon became interested in physics and mathematics.

Galileo experimented with pendulums, levers, balls and other objects. He tried to describe how they moved with mathematical equations. His experimentation led to the invention of the advanced measuring device called the 'hydrostatic balance'. In 1609, having heard of the invention of a telescope, he decided to build his own telescope. He took the archaic telescope and made great improvements to it. Galileo used it extensively to observe outer space. Soon, Galileo's advanced version of the telescope was used throughout Europe. He passed away in Arcetri on 8 January 1642.

IMPORTANT FACT

Galileo made many discoveries using the telescope such as the four large moons around Jupiter and the phases of the planet Venus. He also discovered sunspots and stated that the Moon was not smooth and was, in fact, covered with craters.

31. ISAAC NEWTON

Sir Isaac Newton was an English physicist and mathematician, who is considered to be one of the most influential scientists of all time. He was born on 4 January 1643 in Woolsthorpe, England. After finishing school in 1661, he went to Cambridge University where he concentrated on science, mathematics and philosophy. He read books by Galileo, Rene Descartes, Euclid and Johannes Kepler. He became a professor soon after he graduated from Cambridge around 1669.

The discovery of the gravitational theory is credited to Isaac Newton. He is the one who found a relation between gravity and heavenly bodies in the solar system. He realised that the same relation exists between the earth and the objects on it. After his discovery of gravitational force, Newton elaborated on his theory, giving us the three laws of gravity. Gravity plays a large role in our daily lives and Newton's research has made it easier for us to understand this phenomena. He died on 20 March 1727 in London, England.

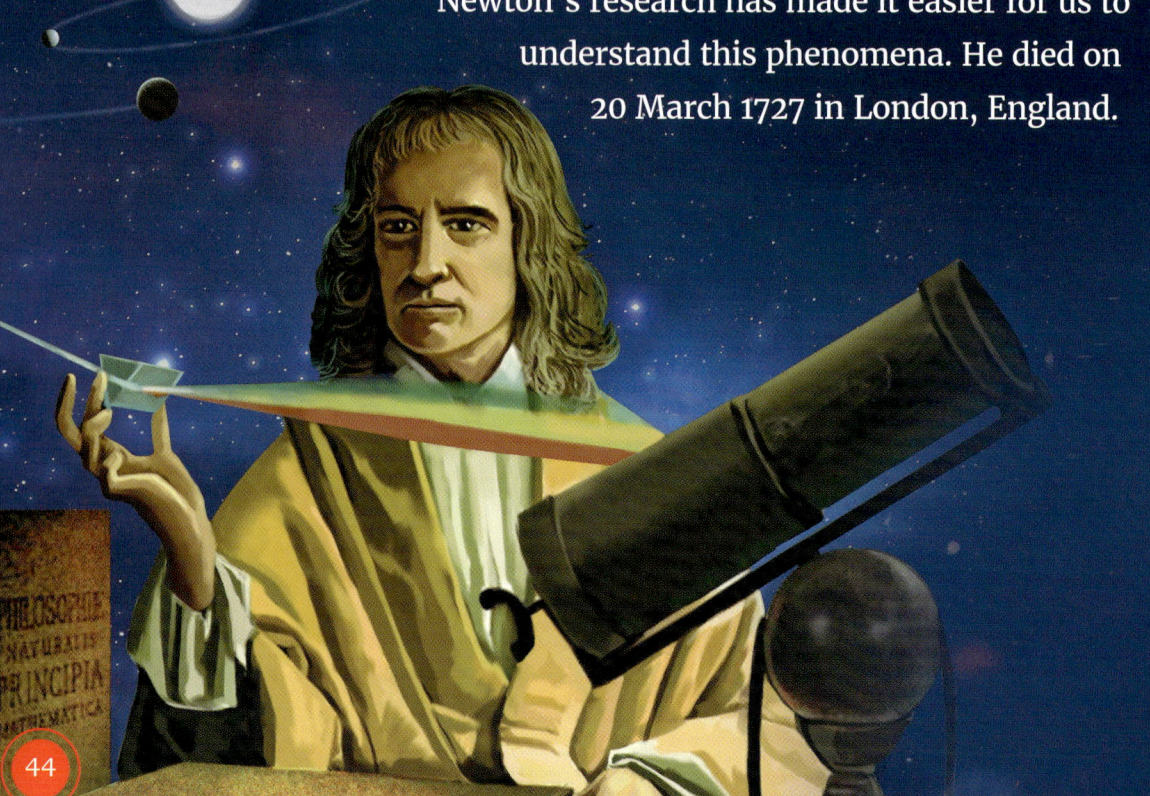

32. BENJAMIN FRANKLIN

Benjamin Franklin was not only one of the founding fathers of the USA, but also a well-renowned printer, scientist, inventor, author, politician and diplomat. He was born on 17 January 1706 in Boston. Even as a child, his passion for reading and experimentation was very intense. He wrote many letters and books.

He suspected that lightning was an electrical current and conducted an experiment to see if it would pass through metal. He invented the lightning rod, Franklin stove and bifocal glasses among other things. He conducted extensive research and published many theories about electricity. He died on 17 April 1790.

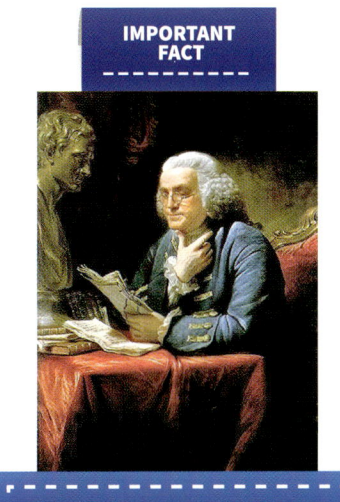

IMPORTANT FACT

Franklin was a fashion icon in France.

33. JAMES WATT

HORSEPOWER

IMPORTANT FACT

WATT COINED THE TERM 'HORSEPOWER' BY DETERMINING THAT A HORSE COULD PULL 180 LBS.

James Watt was a Scottish inventor and mechanical engineer, renowned for his work on the steam engine. He was born on 30 January 1736 in Greenock, Scotland. Watt designed a separate condensing chamber for the steam engine that immensely prevented the loss of power and steam. He received his first patent in 1769 for this device.

By 1790, Watt was an accomplished and wealthy man. He patented several other important inventions including the rotary engine, the double-action engine and the steam indicator. The unit of measurement of electrical and mechanical power, 'Watt', is named in his honour. Watt died on 25 August 1819 in Heathfield, Scotland.

34. CHARLES BABBAGE

IMPORTANT FACT

Babbage's brain on display in the London Science Museum.

Charles Babbage was an English inventor and mathematician, who is also known as the 'father of computers'. He was born in London on 26 December 1791. He was often unwell as a child and was educated mainly at home. He later grew fond of mathematics and went on to pursue it further at Cambridge University in 1810.

In 1820, he invented the 'difference engine', a machine which could perform mathematical calculations. His mathematical machines were based on ideas that were later used in modern computers. He passed away at his home in London on 18 October 1871.

35. LOUIS BRAILLE

Louis Braille was a French educator famous for inventing a system of reading, writing and printing, exclusively for the blind. He was born on 4 January 1809 in Coupvray near Paris, France. He was blinded in an accident when he was three years old. He attended the Royal Institute for Blind Youth, where he studied with raised imprints of letters on an embossed paper. He published his code in which he used six raised dots in different combinations in 1829. He also developed the Braille code for music. He died on 6 January 1852.

Braille is not a language

IMPORTANT FACT

It's a common misconception that Braille is a language. There is a Braille code for almost every foreign language you can imagine! Even math, computer science and music—all have their own unique Braille systems.

36. CHARLES DARWIN

Charles Robert Darwin was a British scientist and naturalist who proposed the theory of evolution by natural selection. He was born on 12 February 1809 in Shrewsbury, England. Darwin went to the University of Edinburgh Medical School to study medicine and later to Cambridge University where he interacted with many naturalists.

Charles Darwin formulated his theory of evolution around 1838 and worked on it for 20 years privately. Darwin's *Theory of Evolution* stated that all life forms are related to and descended from a common ancestor. Another naturalist, Alfred Russel Wallace wrote to him with similar theories. Then the two collaborated and published their theories in 1858. Darwin passed away on 19 April 1882.

Darwin did not coin the phrase 'Survival of the Fittest'

That was Herbert Spencer, a philosopher and contemporary of Charles Darwin. Darwin himself used the phrase in his 5th edition of the Origin and gave full credit to Spencer.

37. THOMAS EDISON

Thomas Alva Edison was a scientist and inventor who pioneered several significant inventions. He was born on 11 February 1847 in Ohio, USA. Edison began working at the young age of 13. By the age of 16, he was working as a telegraph operator. He soon became interested in communications, which was the focus of many of his inventions.

Edison is most well-known for inventing the phonograph, the electric light bulb and the motion picture. He invented ways of producing electricity and distributing it through wires. Edison power stations were all over the world by the 1890s. He passed away on 18 October 1931 in West Orange, New Jersey.

Edison Power Station

IMPORTANT FACT

THE DYNAMO ROOM IN THE FIRST EDISON ELECTRIC LIGHTING STATION AT PEARL STREET IN LOWER MANHATTAN IN 1882

38. ALEXANDER GRAHAM BELL

Alexander Graham Bell was an influential scientist, engineer and inventor. He was born on 3 March 1847 in Edinburgh, Scotland. He is widely credited with the invention of the first practical telephone. His mother and wife were both deaf, which had a major influence on his work. He also had a strong interest in other scientific fields such as developing the photophone, conducting medical research and searching for alternative fuel sources. He passed away on 2 August 1922.

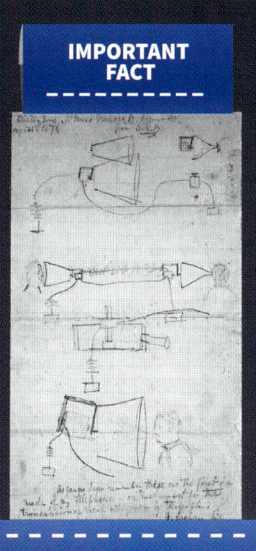

IMPORTANT FACT

Alexander Graham Bell telephone diagram

39. NIKOLA TESLA

Nikola Tesla was a famous electrical engineer, futurist and inventor, who is best known for his design of the modern electrical supply system. He was born on 10 July 1856 in modern day Croatia. Tesla studied in Austria and went to America to work with Thomas Edison.

Tesla's most renowned invention was the 'Tesla coil' in 1891, which is still used in radio technology. Tesla was also a pioneer in the discovery of radar and X-ray technology. Though his patents earned him a lot of money, he spent a lot on experiments too. He died in poverty on 7 January 1943 in New York.

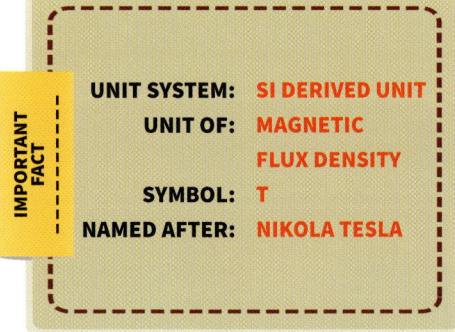

IMPORTANT FACT

UNIT SYSTEM:	SI DERIVED UNIT
UNIT OF:	MAGNETIC FLUX DENSITY
SYMBOL:	T
NAMED AFTER:	NIKOLA TESLA

THE TESLA (SYMBOL T) IS A DERIVED UNIT OF THE STRENGTH OF A MAGNETIC FIELD IN THE INTERNATIONAL SYSTEM OF UNITS.

40. THE WRIGHT BROTHERS

Brothers Wilbur and Orville Wright were inventors and pioneers in the aviation industry. Wilbur was born in Millville, Indiana, on 16 April 1867 and Orville was born in Dayton, Ohio, on 19 August 1871. They went to high school but did not get their diplomas. On 17 December 1903, the Wright brothers launched their first successful air flight in Kitty Hawk.

They were the first to make a successful aircraft that was powered by an engine. They received a patent for their design in 1906.

IMPORTANT FACT

AFTER FOUR FLIGHTS IN THE WRIGHT FLYER ON DECEMBER 17 1903 THE CRAFT NEVER FLEW AGAIN. THIS WAS BECAUSE OF A SUDDEN STRONG GUST OF WIND THAT FLIPPED THE FLYER SEVERAL TIMES, DAMAGING IT HEAVILY.

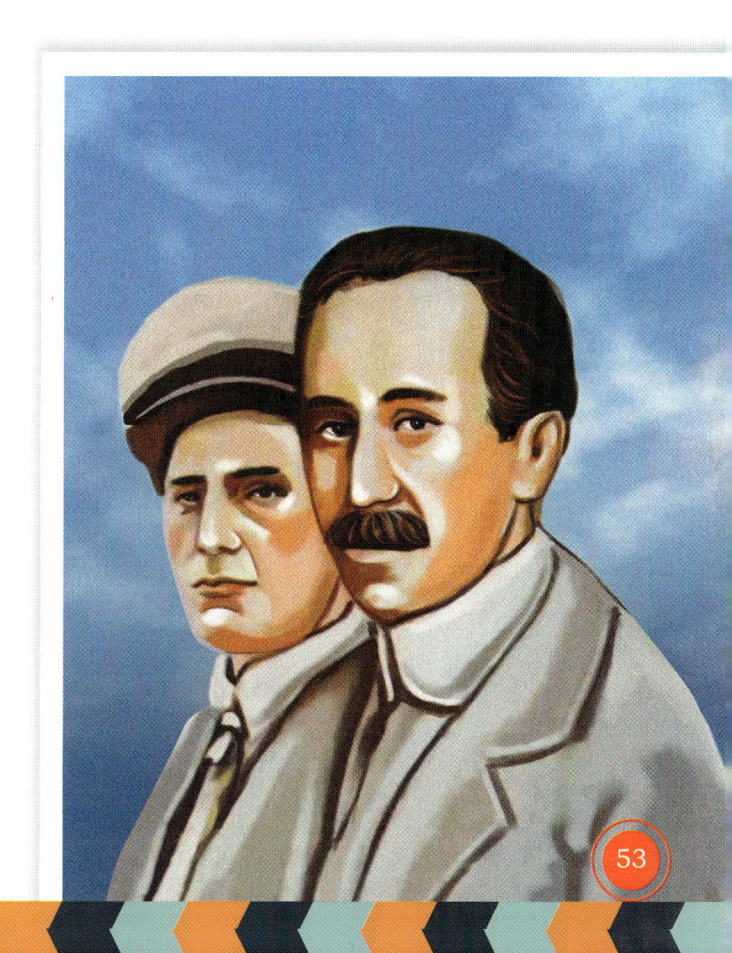

41. GUGLIELMO MARCONI

Guglielmo Marconi was a physicist and inventor who was best known for his work on radio transmission. He was born on 25 April 1874 in Bologna, Italy. Marconi began experimenting with electromagnetics as a student at the Livorno Technical Institute. He developed a system of wireless telegraphy for which he received his first patent in England.

He was awarded the Nobel Prize in Physics with Karl Ferdinand Braun for their development of practical wireless telegraphy. His development of a radio telegraph system led to the establishment of many associated wireless inventions. He died in Rome on 20 July 1937.

IMPORTANT FACT

Marconi was the *first inventor-entrepreneur* to win a Nobel Prize. The Nobel Committee had never before awarded the prize for a practical application rather than theoretical accomplishments.

42. ALBERT EINSTEIN

German genius, Albert Einstein, was born on 14 March 1879 in Ulm, Germany. He had exceptional insight into physics and mathematics. Two things sparked his interest in the sciences. One was a compass that his father gave him when he was ten years old. The other was a geometry book he found when he was twelve. Soon after he graduated, Einstein worked in a patent office evaluating patents for electromagnetic devices.

He worked on many influential theories and projects. Einstein came up with theories about light, matter, gravity, space and time. Einstein is more than just a world-famous scientist; his name represents intelligence and knowledge! In 1921, he received the Nobel Prize for his achievements in theoretical physics. He is best known for developing the theory of relativity. He is regarded as one of the most brilliant minds of the 20th century. He died on 18 April 1955.

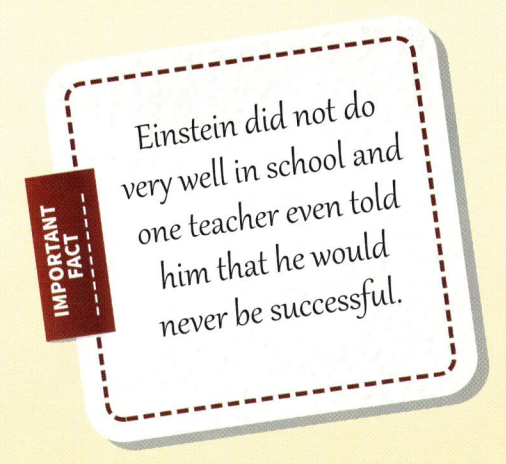

IMPORTANT FACT

Einstein did not do very well in school and one teacher even told him that he would never be successful.

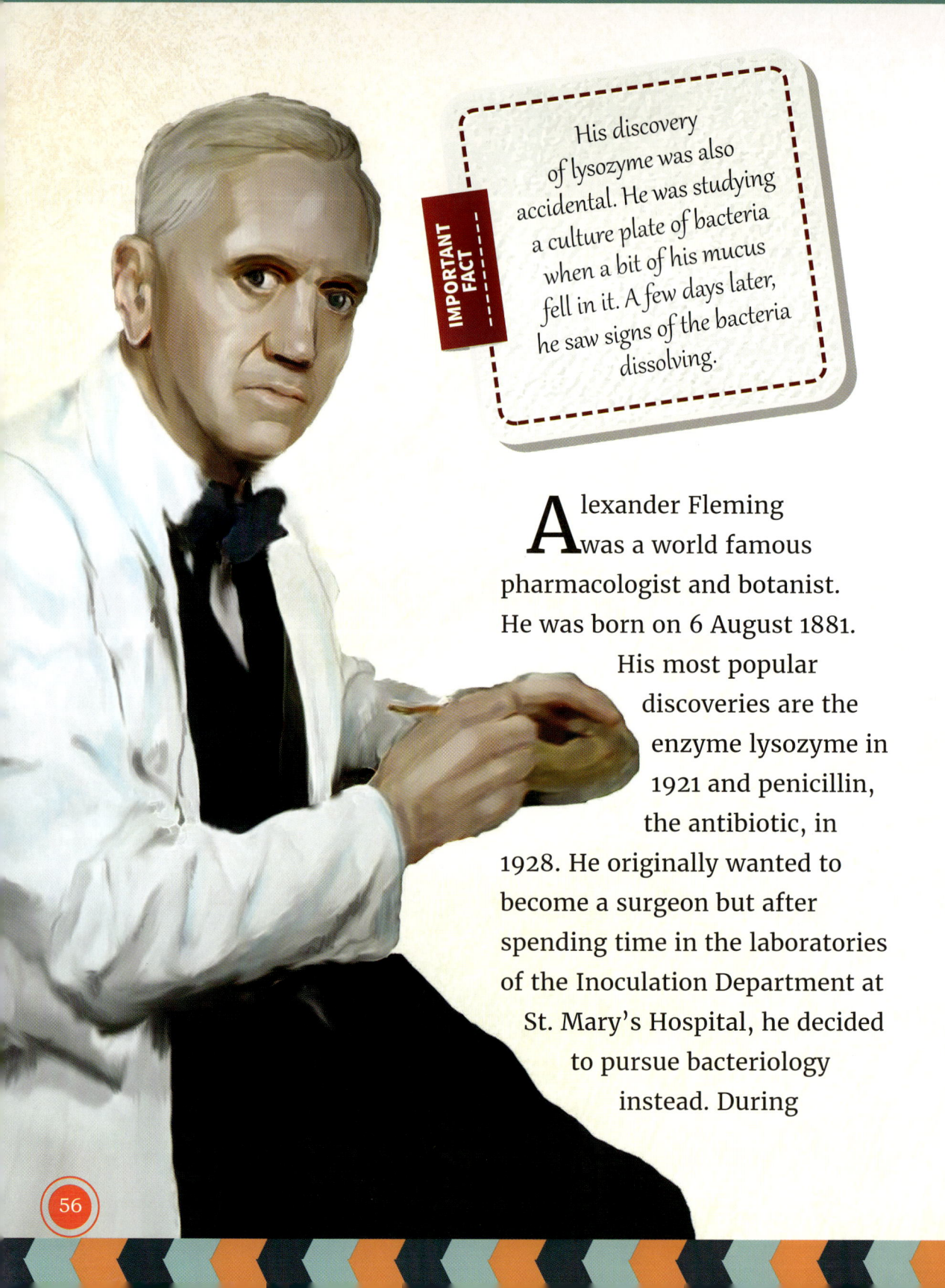

43. ALEXANDER FLEMING

IMPORTANT FACT

His discovery of lysozyme was also accidental. He was studying a culture plate of bacteria when a bit of his mucus fell in it. A few days later, he saw signs of the bacteria dissolving.

Alexander Fleming was a world famous pharmacologist and botanist. He was born on 6 August 1881. His most popular discoveries are the enzyme lysozyme in 1921 and penicillin, the antibiotic, in 1928. He originally wanted to become a surgeon but after spending time in the laboratories of the Inoculation Department at St. Mary's Hospital, he decided to pursue bacteriology instead. During

World War I, he worked as a bacteriologist with the Royal Army Medical Corps and studied soldiers' wounds. He discovered that using strong antiseptics on wounds actually did more harm than good.

In 1928, Fleming made an accidental discovery from a contaminated petri dish. The contaminated bacteria contained a powerful antibiotic, which was later called penicillin. Penicillin stops the growth of harmful bacteria that is responsible for many other dangerous diseases. He, along with two other scientists, received a Nobel Prize for his discovery in 1945. Fleming saved millions of lives with his accidental discovery. He passed away on 11 March 1955.

IMPORTANT FACT

PENICILLIUM FUNGI WERE ORIGINALLY DISCOVERED BY A MEDICAL STUDENT, ERNEST DUCHESNE IN THE LATE 19TH CENTURY, AND THEN RE-DISCOVERED BY ALEXANDER FLEMING IN 1928, FOR ITS ANTIBIOTIC PROPERTIES. ALEXANDER FLEMING REALISED THIS WHEN A SAMPLE OF STAPHYLOCOCCUS, A BACTERIA THAT HE WAS STUDYING, GOT INFECTED BY SOME MOLD AND ALL BACTERIA CELLS CLOSEST TO THE MOLD WERE PERISHING. WITH FURTHER TESTING, FLEMING LEARNT THE MOLD WAS ACTUALLY CREATING A BACTERIA-DEMOLISHING SUBSTANCE, WHICH HE NAMED PENICILLIN.

44. STEPHEN HAWKING

Stephen William Hawking was an English physicist, cosmologist and author. He was born on 8 January 1942 in Oxford, England. He completed his schooling in England and went to Oxford University for higher studies.

He moved to Cambridge University to carry out research in Cosmology. When he returned home after his first term at Cambridge, he experienced clumsiness and a slight speech impediment. Shortly after his 21st birthday, he was diagnosed with an incurable form of a motor neurone disease. Doctors initially gave Hawking two years to live. He began using a wheelchair and eventually lost his power of speech.

He is most well-known for his contribution on the 'Big Bang Theory' and the discovery of 'Black Holes'. He completed his PhD and enjoyed a career as a leading theoretical physicist. In 1979, he was appointed as the Lucasian Professor of Mathematics at Cambridge, the most famous academic chair in the world. Hawking died on 14 March 2018 at Cambridge.

IMPORTANT FACT

In 1974, Hawking was inducted into the Royal Society, a worldwide fellowship of scientists. He was awarded the Eddington Medal from the Royal Astronomical Society. He prided himself for making his complex physical concepts accessible to the common public by writing the bestseller, *A Brief History of Time*.

Legendary Leaders

There are some people who have shaped history and consequently the present. Some of them were revolutionary in the way they led their nation, some were great leaders for different reasons and some were just downright evil in their outlook. But their influence and leadership cannot be denied. Read on to find out more about these legendary leaders.

45. ALEXANDER THE GREAT

Prince Alexander III of Macedonia is known as Alexander the Great. He was born on 20 July 356 BCE in Pella, Macedonia. He was educated by the famous philosopher Aristotle.

He set out to conquer the massive Persian Empire. Against overwhelming odds, he led his army to victories across the Persian territories of Asia, Syria and Egypt, without suffering a single defeat. He founded more than 70 cities throughout the Mediterranean region and west up to India, spreading trade and the Greek culture wherever he went. He passed away at the young age of 32 in 324 BCE.

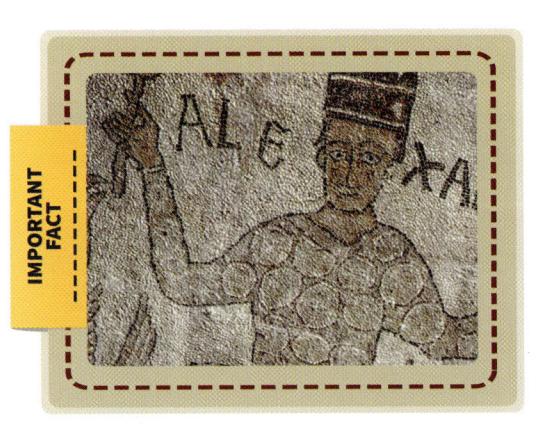

IMPORTANT FACT

AFTER DEFEATING THE PERSIANS, ALEXANDER STARTED DRESSING LIKE THEM. REALISING THAT THE BEST WAY TO MAINTAIN CONTROL OF THE PERSIANS WAS TO ACT LIKE ONE, ALEXANDER BEGAN TO WEAR THE STRIPED TUNIC, GIRDLE AND DIADEM OF PERSIAN ROYAL DRESS—TO THE DISMAY OF CULTURAL PURISTS BACK IN MACEDONIA.

46. JULIUS CAESAR

Julius Caesar was a famous Roman general, statesman and author. He was born in Rome around 100 BCE to an aristocratic family. He became the head of his family at the young age of sixteen after his father passed away. Julius Caesar joined the Roman Army in 81 BCE and was the first Roman to invade England in 55 BCE and again in 54 BCE.

In 65 BCE, Caesar was appointed an 'adele', which put him in charge of Rome's public entertainment. He became very popular among the Romans. Soon after, Caesar joined the army and left Rome in order to avoid Sulla, the dictator of Rome and his allies.

When Sulla died, Caesar returned to Rome in about 46 BCE. He was a military hero from his years in the army and he quickly rose up the ranks of the Roman government. He made significant changes in Rome by constructing new buildings and temples. He soon became the most powerful man in Europe as the Senate made him the dictator. He was assassinated on 15 March 44 BCE.

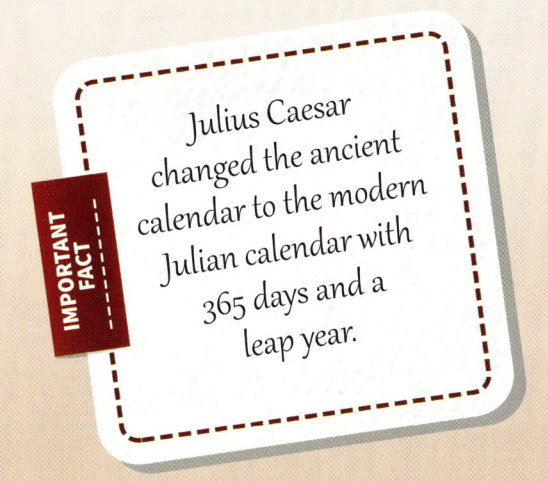

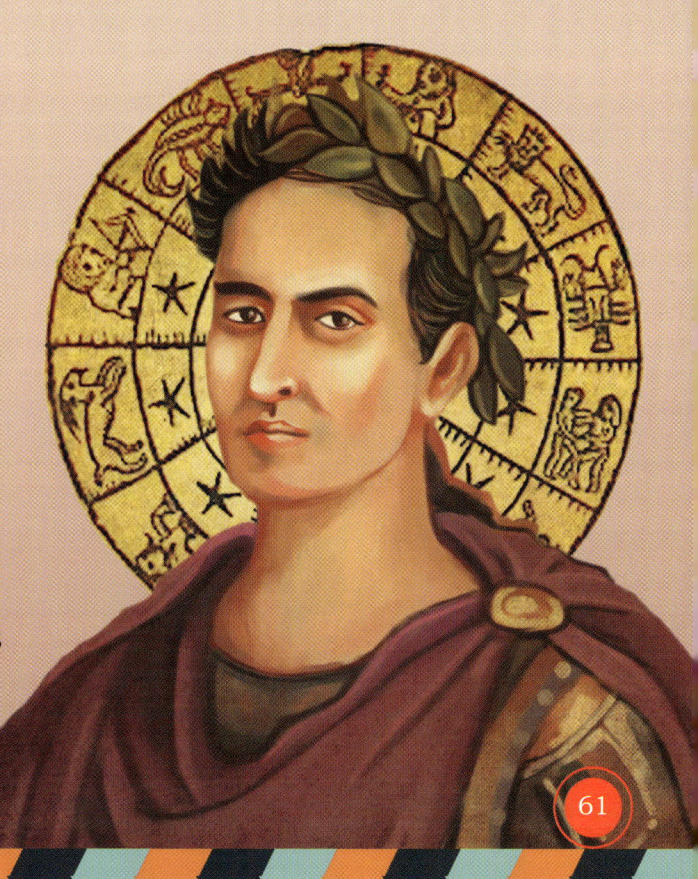

IMPORTANT FACT

Julius Caesar changed the ancient calendar to the modern Julian calendar with 365 days and a leap year.

47. CONSTANTINE

Constantine the Great is one of history's most popular leaders. He was born in 272 CE in modern Serbia. He was well-educated.

He was the first Roman emperor to follow Christianity. He laid the foundation for the growth of western medieval culture. He ruled from 306–337 CE. While he ruled the Eastern Roman Empire, he chose as his capital the small town of Byzantium, which he renamed Constantinople. Constantinople remained the seat of the Eastern Roman Empire until 1453. He passed away in 337 CE.

IMPORTANT FACT

THE ARCH OF CONSTANTINE WAS BUILT TO COMMEMORATE CONSTANTINE'S VICTORY OVER MAXENTIUS AT THE BATTLE OF MILVIAN BRIDGE. THE ARCH OF CONSTANTINE IS THE LARGEST SURVIVING ROMAN TRIUMPHAL ARCH AND THE LAST GREAT MONUMENT OF IMPERIAL ROME. CONSTANTINE THE GREAT WAS THE SECOND LONGEST SERVING ROMAN EMPEROR

48. JOAN OF ARC

Joan d'Arc also known as 'Joan of Arc' or the 'Maid of Orleans' was a Roman Catholic saint who believed she was working under divine guidance. She was born around 1412 in Domrémy, France. She was a peasant girl who had mystical visions about her leadership in a battle between the French and the English.

Joan of Arc was captured during battle at the city of Compiegne. She was executed by the English at the young age of 19 on 30 May 1431.

IMPORTANT FACT

Joan, though remembered as a fearless warrior and considered a heroine of the Hundred Years' War between France and England, never actually fought in battle or killed an opponent.

49. LORENZO DE' MEDICI

IMPORTANT FACT

The Medici family is known as the 'Godfathers of the Renaissance'.

Lorenzo de' Medici or 'Lorenzo the Magnificent' was an Italian statesman and Florentine's famous ruler and patron during the Italian Renaissance. He was born on 1 January 1449 in Florence, Italy. He ruled Florence initially with his brother Giuliano and on his own after his brother's assassination. He was best known for his patronage of the arts. Those under his protection included great Renaissance artists such as Botticelli and Leonardo da Vinci. He passed away on 9 April 1492.

50. HENRY VIII

Henry VIII was the King of England. He presided over the initial stages of the English Renaissance and the English Reformation. He was born on 28 June 1491 in England. He excelled at book learning and physical activities as a child.

He was appointed Duke of York and Lord Lieutenant of Ireland while he was still a child. In 1501, he was appointed as the Prince of Wales. In 1509, when Henry was eighteen years old, he succeeded the throne after his father's death. He died at the age of 56 in 1547.

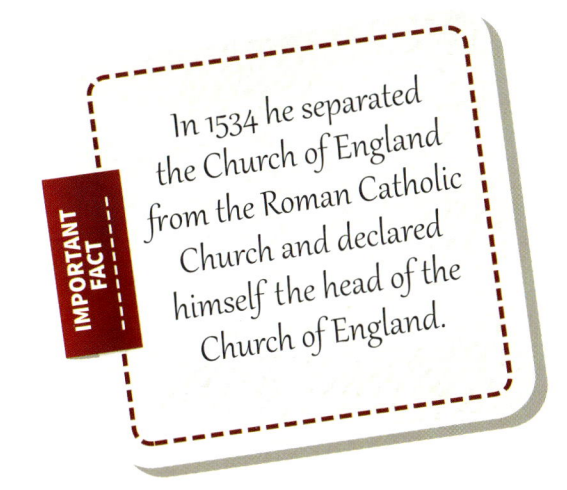

IMPORTANT FACT

In 1534 he separated the Church of England from the Roman Catholic Church and declared himself the head of the Church of England.

51. QUEEN ELIZABETH I

Queen Elizabeth I was the fifth and last monarch of the Tudor Dynasty of England. She was born on 7 September 1533 in Greenwich, England and was crowned Queen of England on 15 January 1559. Because she never married or had children, she was also called 'Virgin Queen'.

Highly educated, Elizabeth I turned her court into a centre for learning. She also strengthened the currency and promoted government reforms, leading to a growth of the economy.

Elizabeth's 45-year reign is known as the Elizabethan Age, during which England became a strong European power. She died on 24 March 1603 in Richmond, England.

IMPORTANT FACT

Before she was queen, Elizabeth 1 was a political prisoner.

52. THOMAS JEFFERSON

Thomas Jefferson, the third president of the USA was also one of its seven Founding Fathers. He was the main author of the Declaration of Independence. He was born on 13 April 1743 in Shadwell, Virginia. Jefferson was an obsessive student who daily spent more than fifteen hours with his books on a regular basis.

In 1775, Jefferson was elected to the Continental Congress to write the Declaration of Independence which states that 'all men are created equal'. The Declaration also states the reasons the colonists wanted to separate from England. He passed away on 4 July 1826.

IMPORTANT FACT: Thomas Jefferson wrote his own epitaph and designed the grave marker.

53. ABRAHAM LINCOLN

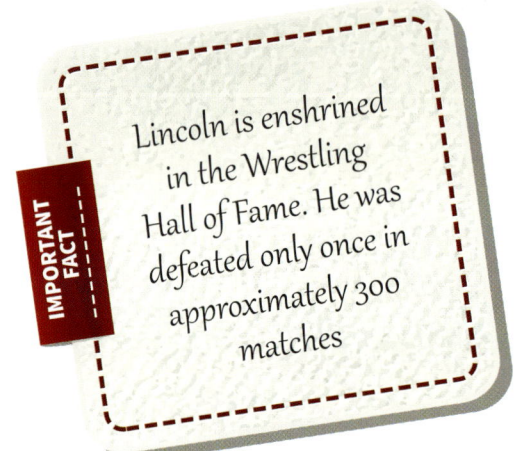

IMPORTANT FACT: Lincoln is enshrined in the Wrestling Hall of Fame. He was defeated only once in approximately 300 matches

Abraham Lincoln has been ranked among the most influential American Presidents. He was born on 12 February 1809 in Kentucky, USA. Despite very little formal schooling he educated himself to be a lawyer.

He was the 16th President of the USA. He successfully led his country through its worst constitutional and moral crisis—the American Civil War. In 1863, he issued the law and proclaimed the freedom of slaves in the Southern states. Gradually, slavery was banned all over America and all slaves were freed. He was assassinated in 1865 in Washington DC.

54. THEODORE ROOSEVELT

Theodore Roosevelt was a soldier and a writer who became the 26th President of the USA. He was born on 27 October 1858 in New York. He was educated by private tutors and was a very intelligent child.

When the Spanish War broke out in 1898, he formed a voluntary group of soldiers who called themselves 'Rough Riders'. They became famous after their victorious fight in Cuba. He served as the American President from 1901–1909. He worked hard to improve the quality of life for the average American. He died on 6 January 1919.

IMPORTANT FACT

Theodore Roosevelt won the Nobel Peace Prize for his role in mediating the Treaty of Portsmouth, which ended the Russo-Japanese War.

55. MAHATMA GANDHI

Mohandas Karamchand Gandhi was one of the most famous freedom fighters of the Indian Nationalist Movement against the British. He was born on 2 October 1869 in Porbander, Gujarat, India. He is fondly remembered as Mahatma Gandhi. He studied law in England and took up a job as a lawyer in South Africa.

On his return to India, he followed non-violent methods of protests like fasts and marches against the British rule. The 'Quit India Movement' initiated by him was a great success and India became independent on 15 August 1947. He was assassinated on 30 January 1948.

IMPORTANT FACT

In 1930, Mohandas Gandhi was named 'Man of the Year' by Time Magazine. Now this coveted title is popularly known as the 'Time Person of the Year'. No other Indian has ever been Time's Person of the Year since then.

56. WINSTON CHURCHILL

Winston Churchill was a British author, statesman and politician who served as Britain's Prime Minister during World War II. He was born on 30 November 1874 in Oxfordshire, England. Churchill had a poor academic record due to which his father made him join the army. He became popular as a journalist while he reported his travels to Spain during the Cuban War of Independence and his visit to British India.

Churchill won a seat to the British Parliament in 1900 and became the Prime Minister in 1940. His leadership during World War II enabled the British Empire to stand against Hitler and the Germans. Churchill led Britain from the brink of defeat to victory. He served his country for many years. Churchill authored many books, some of which are *History of the English-Speaking Peoples*, *The Second World War*, *Savrola* and *The River War*. Churchill was also awarded the Nobel Prize for Literature. Churchill resigned from active politics in 1955. He died on 24 January 1965.

IMPORTANT FACT

Winston Churchill was an amateur painter who painted more than 600 paintings in his lifetime.

57. JOHN F. KENNEDY

John Fitzgerald Kennedy was the 35th President of the USA. He was born on 29 May 1917 in Massachusetts, USA. He grew up in a powerful political family in Brookline, Massachusetts. In September 1941, Kennedy joined the US Navy. After the loss of his brother and brother-in-law, who were both defending their country, John ran for Congress in the early 1950s and won.

Kennedy ran for presidency in 1960 against then Vice President Richard Nixon. He won in one of the closest elections in history. He served as President from 1961 to 1963 until his assassination. He was assassinated in Texas on 22 November 1963.

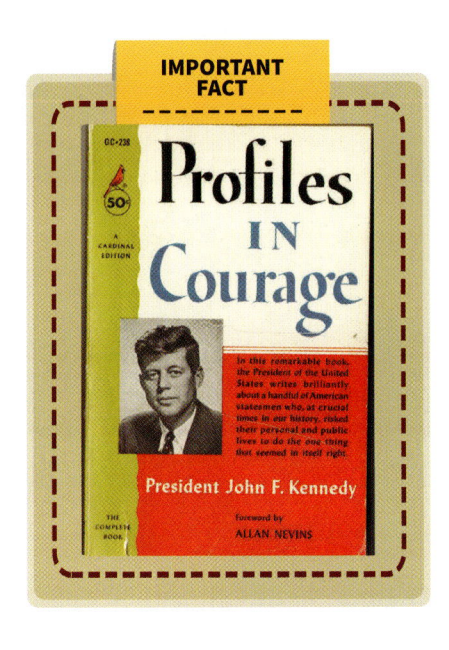

IMPORTANT FACT

A PULITZER PRIZE IN BIOGRAPHY WAS AWARDED TO PRESIDENT J F KENNEDY FOR 'PROFILES IN COURAGE'. THERE HAS SINCE BEEN CONTROVERSY AS TO HOW MUCH OF THE BOOK WAS GHOSTWRITTEN BY HIS AIDE, THEODORE SORENSEN.

58. MARGARET THATCHER

Margaret Thatcher the 'Iron Lady', was the first woman Prime Minister of Britain. She was born on 13 October 1925 in Lincolnshire, England. She studied chemistry from Oxford University and also practised as a barrister from 1954. Thatcher had great interest in politics.

Thatcher ran for the Parliament in 1950 but was not successful. She was elected to the House of Commons in 1959 and worked her way up the ranks. Thatcher was elected as the Prime Minister in 1975. She was the only British Prime Minister of the 20th century to have held office for three consecutive terms. Thatcher introduced many social and political reforms to tackle unemployment. She stated that the individual should not be completely bound by the state and advocated privatisation of state owned enterprises, sale of public houses to tenants, limits on the amount of money printed, etc. Thatcher announced her resignation as Prime Minister in November 1990, but continued to influence national politics. She passed away on 8 April 2013 in London.

IMPORTANT FACT

All of Margaret Thatcher's theories, combined with her personal look and style, came to be known as Thatcherism. She was one of the most dominant political figures of 20th century Britain.

59. INDIRA GANDHI

Indira Gandhi was an Indian politician who served as Prime Minister for three consecutive terms and started a fourth term that ended abruptly with her assassination. She was born on 19 November 1917 in Allahabad, India. Indira Gandhi studied at Visva Bharati University in West Bengal and then at Oxford University in the UK. She joined the Congress Party in 1938. In 1942, she married Feroze Gandhi, a member of the Congress party. They had two children, Sanjay and Rajiv.

The Congress Party came to power in 1947 when her father assumed office as Prime Minister and she became a member of its working committee in 1955. Later, she was elected to the largely honorary post of party president. She was made a member of the Rajya Sabha in 1964 and that year, She was also named Minister of Information and Broadcasting. She brought about a remarkable change in the country's economic, political, international and national policies. She was assassinated on 31 October 1984 in New Delhi, India.

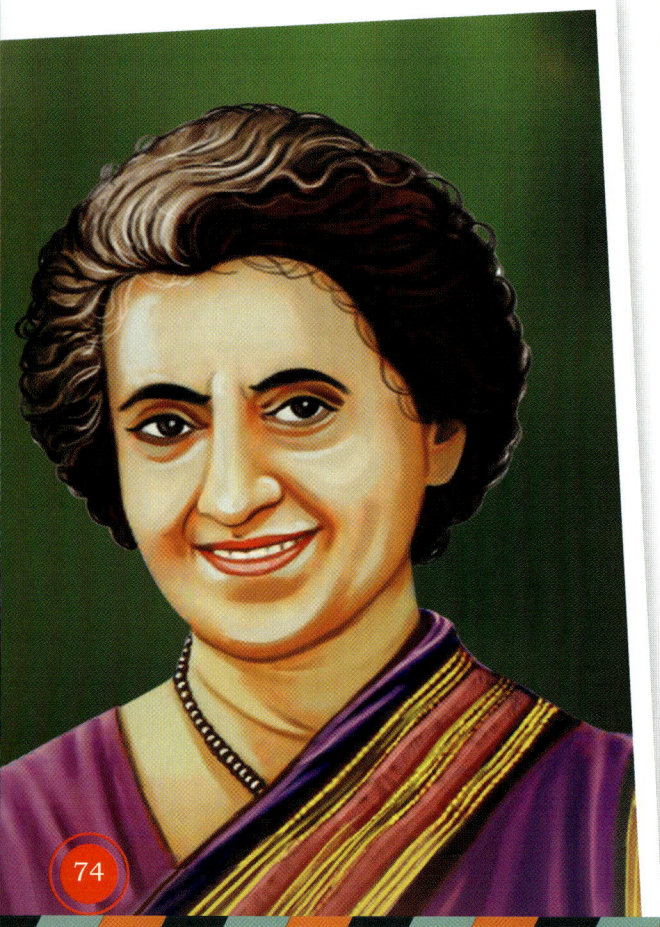

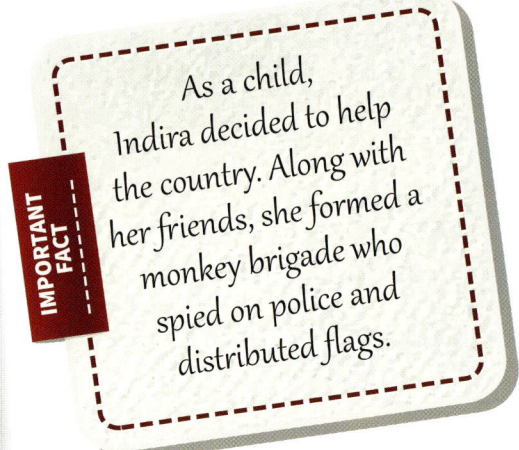

IMPORTANT FACT
As a child, Indira decided to help the country. Along with her friends, she formed a monkey brigade who spied on police and distributed flags.

60. MARTIN LUTHER KING JR.

Martin Luther King Jr. was an American activist and humanitarian who was the leader of the African-American Civil Rights Movement. He was born on 15 January 1929 in Georgia, USA. King earned a bachelor's degree in sociology and divinity. He finished his PhD from Boston University.

Martin Luther King Jr. experienced racism when he was young and decided to do something to end it. He worked towards racial equality and equal rights for all in the USA. He was assassinated at the young age of 39 on 4 April 1968.

IMPORTANT FACT

The civil rights leader was born Michael King Jr. on January 15 1929. In 1934, his father traveled to Germany and became inspired by the Protestant Reformation leader Martin Luther. As a result, King Sr. changed his own name as well as that of his 5-year-old son.

61. BENAZIR BHUTTO

Benazir Bhutto, a Pakistani politician, was the first woman leader of a Muslim nation in modern history. She was born on 21 June 1953. She served two terms as Prime Minister, one in 1988–1990 and the other in 1993–1996. She studied at Harvard University, graduating in 1973. She endured frequent house arrests between 1979 and 1984 and was even exiled for two years from 1984–1986. She returned to Pakistan after her exile. She was assassinated on 27 December 2007.

Lights, Camera, Action!

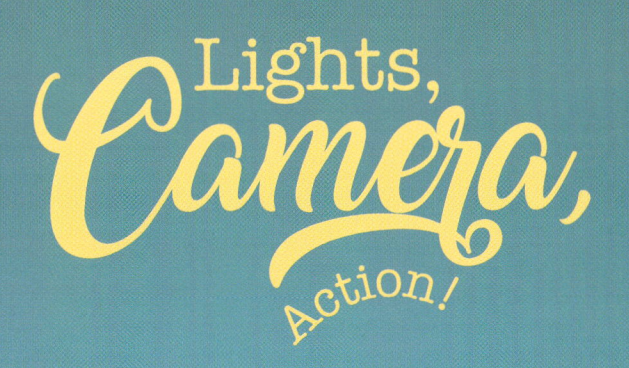

Some people have shaped history and consequently the present. Some of them were revolutionary in the way they led their nation, some were great leaders for different reasons and some were just downright evil in their outlook. But their influence and leadership cannot be denied. Read on to find out more about these legendary leaders.

62. CHARLIE CHAPLIN

Sir Charles Spencer Chaplin was a British producer, writer, director and comedian, who is considered to be the greatest comic artist in the history of world cinema. He was born on 16 April 1889 in London, England. Chaplin's childhood was filled with hardships and he was sent to many workhouses as his mother was sent to a medical asylum.

Chaplin became a professional entertainer when he joined Eight Lancashire Lads, a clog dancing troupe. He also worked as a stage actor for some time. Chaplin joined the Fred Karno Company in 1908 and became famous for his work in '*A Night in an English Music Hall*'. While on tour in America, he got an opportunity to work for Keystone comedy films. Although the first film was not a great success, it was the second film—'*Kid Auto Races at Venice*', where Charlie Chaplin improvised on his character and his immortal screen character 'The Little Tramp' was born. Charlie Chaplin made great films like *The Kid*, *The Gold Rush*, and *The Great Dictator*, among others. He died on 25 December 1977.

> **IMPORTANT FACT**
> Charlie Chaplin was the first actor to have had a comic strip made on him and also the first actor to have appeared on the cover of the Time magazine.

63. WALT DISNEY

Walter Elias Disney was an American filmmaker, producer, businessman and pioneer of animated cartoon films. Not only did he start Walt Disney Productions, he also planned and built Disneyland, the huge amusement park in Los Angeles, California. Disney was born on 5 December 1901 in Chicago, Illinois, USA.

Disney was an innovator of animation. He shot to fame with his creation of the cheerful and mischievous Mickey Mouse. He went on to create more famous characters like Minnie Mouse, Donald Duck and many more.

The clever use of music and sound in his cartoons is what made Disney successful all over the world during the 1930s. The Disney Company is now one of the world's largest entertainment companies.

During his lifetime, Disney won 22 Academy Awards and received four honorary Academy Awards. He won seven Emmy Awards. He died on 15 December 1966.

IMPORTANT FACT: Walt Disney himself was the first voice of Mickey Mouse!

64. WARNER BROTHERS

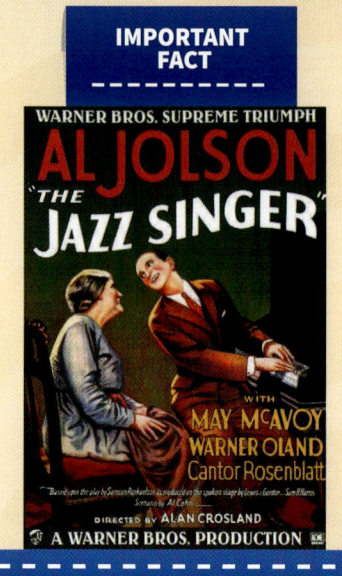

IMPORTANT FACT

The first feature length talking movie, 'The Jazz Singer' was produced by Warner Brothers.

Albert Warner, Sam Warner, Jack Warner and Harry Warner are the founders of Warner Brothers Entertainment, Inc. Warner Brothers was started in 1923 and since then has become one of the biggest film studios in the world. They are global leaders in feature films and release almost twenty films each year in over 120 countries. Warner Brothers also has a television division which has produced many successful shows.

65. STEVEN SPIELBERG

Steven Allan Spielberg is a filmmaker, director and producer. He was born on 18 December 1946 in Cincinnati, Ohio. He has been one of the most influential and popular filmmakers in cinema for over four decades. He became one of the youngest television directors for Universal in the late 1960s. A highly praised television film, *Duel*, brought him the opportunity to direct for cinema and he is now one of the most commercially successful directors of all time.

His movies range from science fiction to historical dramas. He is famous for movies such as *E.T.: The Extra-Terrestrial* and *Schindler's List*. Three of Spielberg's films achieved box office records, becoming the highest grossing films made. He also won two Academy Awards for *Schindler's List* and *Saving Private Ryan*.

IMPORTANT FACT
Spielberg had his first encounter with Hollywood when he sneaked out of Universal Studio tour and into the studio lot, where he met a helpful editor who showed him the basics of film-making.

66. TIM BURTON

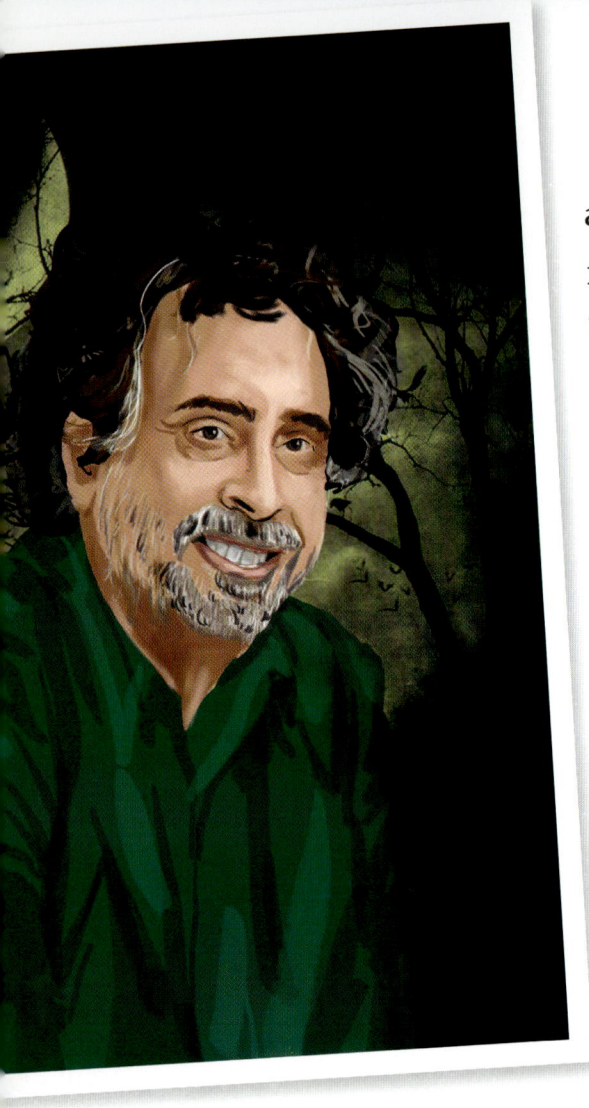

Timothy Walter 'Tim' Burton is a producer, director, writer, poet and stop motion artist, who is famous for his horror and fantasy films. He was born on 25 August 1958 in Burbank, California. He majored in Animation at the California Institute of Arts. Burton is well-known for his blockbuster films like *Edward Scissorhands, Beetlejuice, Alice in Wonderland* and *Charlie and the Chocolate Factory*, among many others. He has also written and published a collection of poems titled *The Melancholy Death of Oyster Boy and Other Stories*. Tim Burton has won one Emmy Award and one Golden Globe Award.

EVERY CHARACTER IN TIM BURTON'S ALICE IN WONDERLAND'S WONDERLAND HAS A PROPER NAME. THE MARCH HARE AND THE CATERPILLAR ARE NAMED THACKERY AND ABSOLEM, RESPECTIVELY, IN THE MOVIE

IMPORTANT FACT

Literary Lords

This section focuses on people whose names have been etched in the list of all time literary greats. Let's find out about their language skills as well as their lives. Read on and get to know these literary lords.

67. DANTE ALIGHIERI

IMPORTANT FACT

Dante Alighieri is called the father of Italian language. That's why the Italian language is called la langue de Dante in French.

IMPORTANT FACT

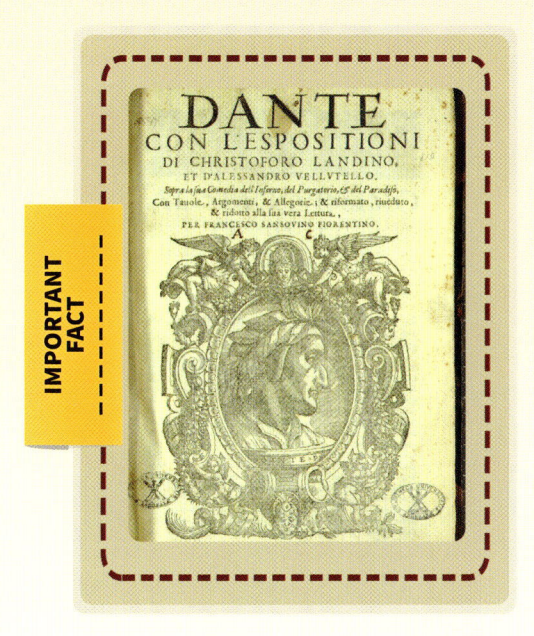

THE DIVINE COMEDY ALSO DRAWS FROM DANTE'S PERSONAL EXPERIENCE OF EXILE FROM HIS NATIVE CITY, FLORENCE.

Dante Alighieri, commonly known as Dante, was an Italian poet, prose writer, political thinker and moral philosopher. He was born in June 1265. He is best known for his epic poem, *The Divine Comedy*. This is a great work of medieval literature and examines philosophical questions of man's eternal destiny.

The poem is written in several sections which represent the three tiers of the Christian afterlife—purgatory, heaven and hell. The poem is often called the greatest literary work composed in Italian.

He made the conscious choice to write this poem in Italian and not Latin, as most scholarly works at that time were written. By doing this, he not only encouraged the common culture of his country, but also paved the way for Italian to become the literary language in Western Europe for many years to come. Dante died in September 1321.

68. WILLIAM SHAKESPEARE

William Shakespeare was an English poet and playwright, widely regarded as the greatest writer and dramatist in the English language. Very little is known about Shakespeare's childhood, except that he was born in England on 23 April 1564. Shakespeare wrote plays that captured the complete range of human emotions and conflict.

He was also an actor. His plays became very popular in London and soon, 'The Lord Chamberlain's Men' were one of the most popular acting companies in the city.

These plays have been performed in countless hamlets, villages, cities and metropolises for more than 400 years. Some of his early plays include *The Taming of the Shrew, Richard III, Romeo and Juliet* and *A Midsummer Night's Dream*.

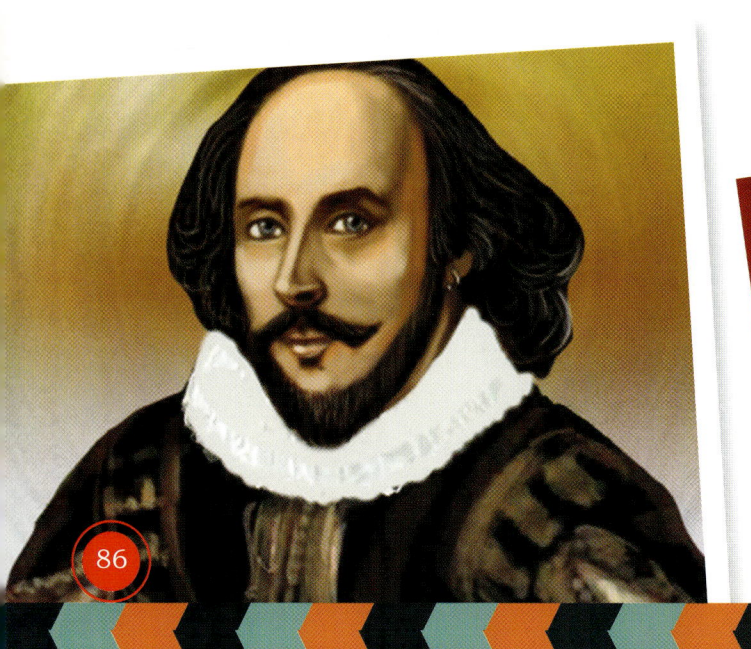

IMPORTANT FACT

During his lifetime, Shakespeare wrote 37 plays and 154 sonnets! This means he produced around one and a half plays a year since he first started writing in 1589.

69. JANE AUSTEN

Jane Austen was a renowned English novelist, famous for her witty satires. She was born on 16 December 1775. She started writing poems, stories and comics in order to amuse her family members. She collected all these into three bound notebooks, which are now called Austen's *Juvenalia*. The novel focuses on courtship and marriage. It is still popular for its portrayal of the English society of the time. They depict her insights into the lives of women during the late 18th century and the early 19th century.

She first started writing around 1787. She wrote many plays, essays and short novels.

Her writing concentrates on the problems of women in those days and was what we would now call feminist in nature.

Some of her famous work includes *Pride and Prejudice, Sense and Sensibility* and *Emma*. She died on 18 July 1817.

> **IMPORTANT FACT**
> Jane Austen was educated by her father, older brothers and through her own reading. Her family supported her writing career, which was very progressive for the time.

70. LEWIS CARROLL

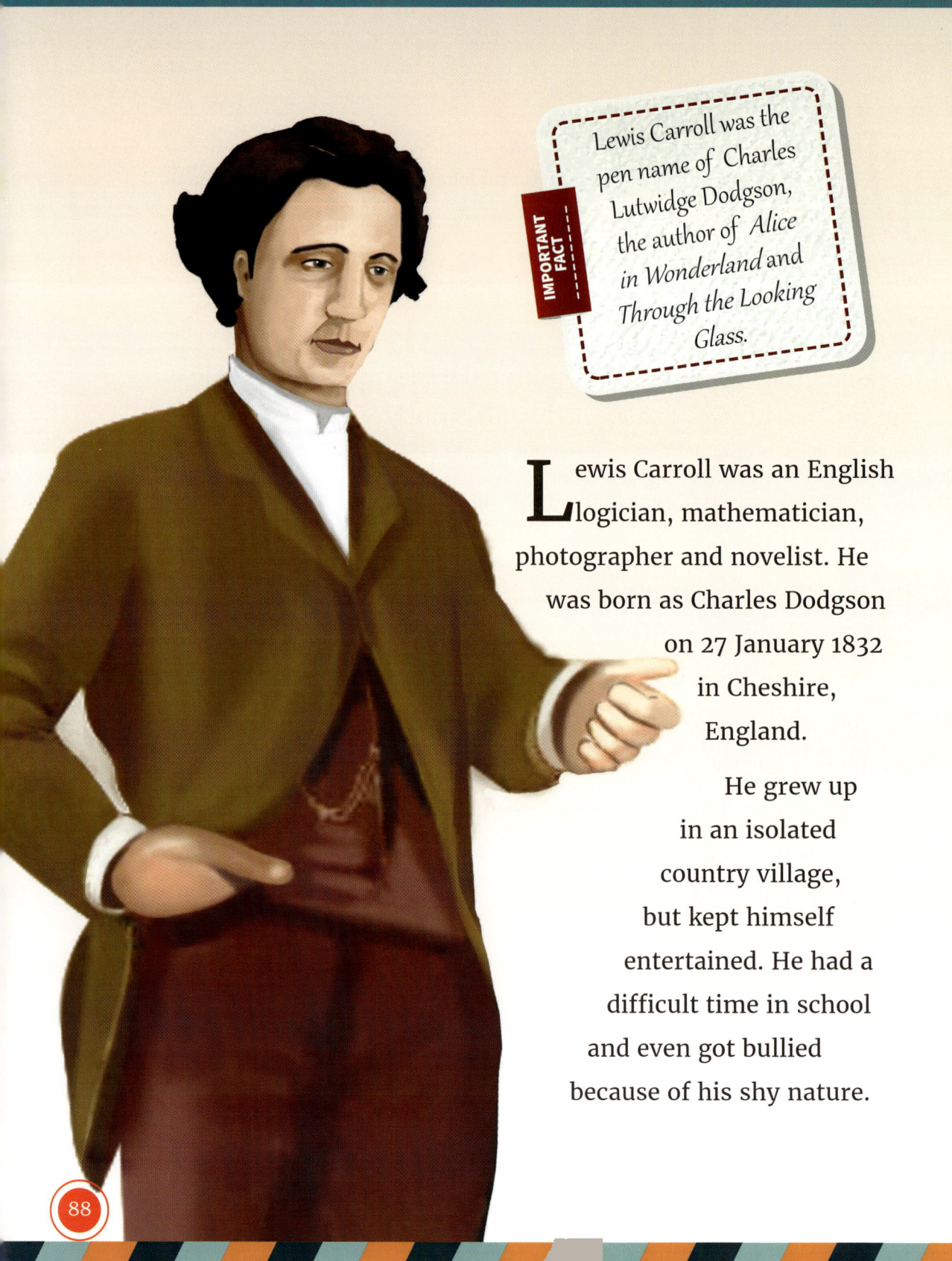

IMPORTANT FACT

Lewis Carroll was the pen name of Charles Lutwidge Dodgson, the author of *Alice in Wonderland* and *Through the Looking Glass*.

Lewis Carroll was an English logician, mathematician, photographer and novelist. He was born as Charles Dodgson on 27 January 1832 in Cheshire, England.

He grew up in an isolated country village, but kept himself entertained. He had a difficult time in school and even got bullied because of his shy nature.

He fell ill as a child and was deaf in one ear for the rest of his life. After schooling, he decided to continue studying. He got a scholarship at Christ Church, Oxford. He was exceptionally good at mathematics and graduated first in his class. He was offered a job and took up teaching at the college.

He would often entertain the dean's children by telling them stories that he would make up. One day, he told them about a little girl named Alice and her adventures underground. It was so good that they asked him to write it down for them. A writer, Henry Kingsley, happened to pick it up and read it. He convinced Carroll to publish it, which he did. It became so popular that he even wrote a sequel, *Through the Looking Glass*. He died on 14 January 1898.

IMPORTANT FACT

LEWIS CARROLL SUFFERED FROM A STAMMER. BUT HE FOUND THAT HE COULD SPEAK FLUENTLY AND NATURALLY TO CHILDREN, WHICH IS WHY HE ENJOYED THEIR COMPANY.

71. ARTHUR CONAN DOYLE

VERY FEW PEOPLE KNOW THAT SIR ARTHUR CONAN DOYLE CAN ACTUALLY BE CREDITED FOR THE *JURASSIC PARK*. HE WROTE *THE LOST WORLD* IN 1912, AT A TIME WHEN PEOPLE HARDLY KNEW WHAT DINOSAURS WERE. HIS BOOK GAINED IMMENSE POPULARITY AND INSPIRED A LOT OF NOVELS AND MOVIES.

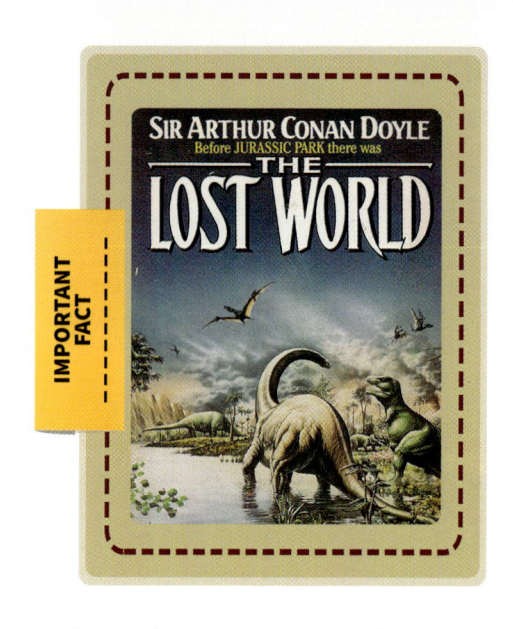

IMPORTANT FACT

Sir Arthur Conan Doyle was a Scottish writer and physician. He was the creator of Sherlock Holmes. He was born on 22 May 1859 in Edinburgh, Scotland. He studied to be a doctor. He settled in Portsmouth where he practised medicine and wrote stories. He first wrote about Sherlock Holmes in *A Study of Scarlet*, published in Beeton's Christmas Annual in 1887. It was a huge success and Doyle wrote more stories about the sleuth. Doyle had a varied career as a writer, journalist and public figure. He died on 7 July 1930.

72. OSCAR WILDE

Oscar Wilde was a gifted poet and playwright, who was very popular in 19th century England. He was born on 16 October 1854. He was very progressive in his thinking and was known to preach the importance of style in life and art. He also attacked the narrow minded Victorian thought. Wilde is best known for his witty plays like *Salome*, *An Ideal Husband* and *The Importance of Being Earnest*. In spite of being a skilled writer, he only wrote one complete novel during his lifetime, *The Picture of Dorian Gray*, published in 1891. He died on 30 November 1900.

IMPORTANT FACT

Oscar Wilde became a contributor of various journals over artistic matters on which he reviewed and commented in a journalistic style. He also become the editor of The Lady's World magazine which he would rename The Woman's World.

73. RABINDRANATH TAGORE

Rabindranath Tagore was a Bengali poet, storywriter, essayist, playwright and artist from India. He was born on 7 May 1861. He was awarded the Nobel Prize for Literature in 1913. He introduced a new form of story writing. He was also famous for using everyday terms in Bengali literature. He studied in England and is known for showcasing Indian art in the West and vice versa. Some of his most famous works are *Sonar Tari* and *Chitrangada*. He has also penned India's national anthem. He died on 7 August 1941.

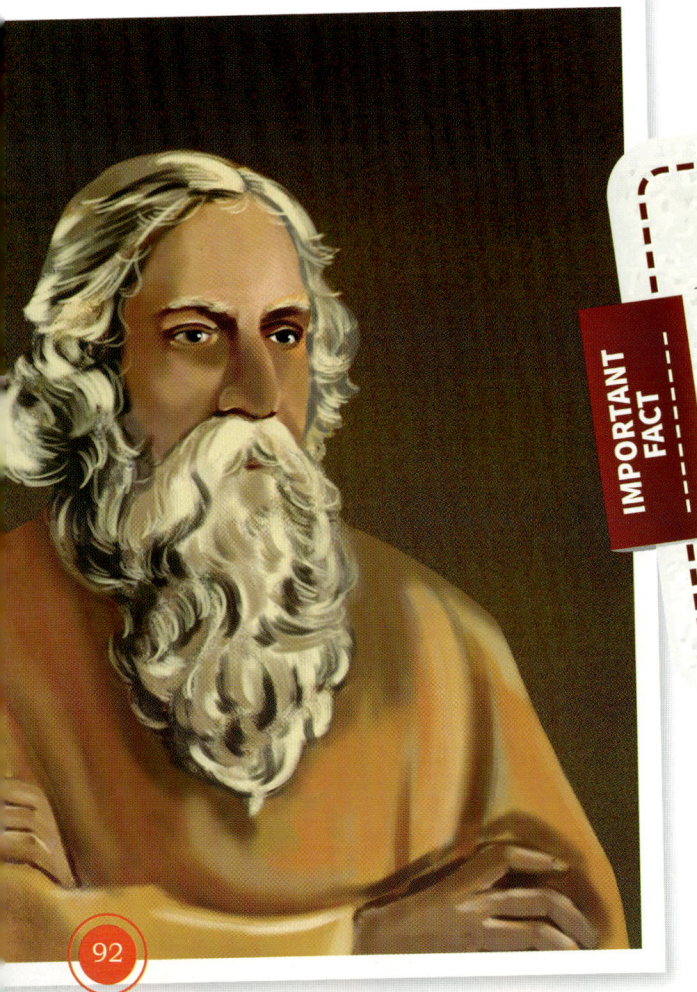

IMPORTANT FACT

Most people know that Tagore wrote the national anthems of India and Bangladesh - 'Jana Gana Mana' and 'Amar Sonar Bangla' respectively. But few know that Sri Lanka's national anthem is based on a Bengali song originally written by Tagore in 1938. It was translated into Sinhalese and adopted as the national anthem in 1951.

74. WILLIAM RANDOLPH HEARST

William Randolph Hearst was a newspaper publisher who built the largest newspaper chain in America. He was born in San Francisco, California, on 29 April 1863. He took over his father's struggling newspaper, San Francisco Examiner, and introduced a sensational style of reporting. Within the next two years, the newspaper was showing a profit. Competition with Pulitzer and the New York World gave rise to what later came to be known as 'yellow journalism' with bold catchy headlines and exaggerated stories. He died on 14 August 1951.

IMPORTANT FACT

Yellow Journalism - a style of journalism coined during the newspaper wars between Hearst and Joseph Pulitzer II (owner of New York World) that include over dramatised and exaggerated stories. This was used to capture the paper's readership and influence public opinion on important topics

75. WILLIAM BUTLER YEATS

William Butler Yeats was an Irish poet and playwright. He was born on 13 June 1865 in Dublin, Ireland. He was one of the most well-known figures of 20th century literature. He made major contributions to both the Irish and the British literary establishments. He later served as an Irish senator for two terms. He was largely responsible for the Irish Literary Revival. He is one of the few writers who delivered their best work after winning a Nobel Prize. Some of these include *The Tower* and *The Winding Stair* and *Other Poems*. He died on 28 January 1939.

IMPORTANT FACT

Willian Butler Yeats co-founded the Abbey Theatre in Dublin

76. J.R.R. TOLKIEN

J.R.R. Tolkien is credited with the revival of fantasy fiction for adults. He was born on 3 January 1892. He was a lecturer of English and literature, specialising in Old and Middle English. He did not write with the intention of getting published. He began writing his first published work, *The Hobbit* as a story for his daughter. When it was published in 1937, it was an instant hit. His publisher asked for a sequel, which he delivered 17 years later. The sequel, *The Lord of the Rings* soon became one of the highest selling books of the 20th century. He died on 2 September 1973.

IMPORTANT FACT

Tolkien heavily revised The Hobbit, especially the scenes between Bilbo and Gollum, to make the story work better with its successor, The Lord of the Rings. These changes were reflected in the second edition, published in 1951 in the US and the UK.

77. F. SCOTT FITZGERALD

Francis Scott Key Fitzgerald was a short story writer, who is considered to be among the greatest 20th century American writers. He was born on 24 September 1896. His first novel, *The Side of Paradise*, was a great success that made him famous. Fitzgerald and his wife Zelda became important social figures. They moved to Paris, where he wrote his most famous novel, *The Great Gatsby* in 1925. His later work was unsuccessful and he moved to Hollywood and became a scriptwriter. He died of a heart attack on 21 December 1940 leaving his last book incomplete.

IMPORTANT FACT

THE GREAT GATSBY SOLD NO MORE THAN 25,000 COPIES IN FITZGERALD'S LIFETIME. IT HAS NOW SOLD OVER 25 MILLION COPIES.

78. ENID BLYTON

Enid Blyton is one of the world's most famous writer of books for children. She was born on 11 August 1897. She was also one of the most prolific writers of all time, writing more than 700 books!

She is popular for her books in which children have adventures with little or no help from adults. Her books are still extremely popular across the world. They have been translated into about 90 languages. As a teenager, her main interest had been writing poems, stories and other items. She had sent many of them to magazines, but none of them got published. She worked as a teacher, and began to have her articles about children and education printed in a magazine called Teachers' World. Her first book of poetry, *Child Whispers* was published in 1922.

Her famous adventure series include *The Famous Five*, *The Secret Seven*, *The Five Find-Outers and Dog*, *St. Claires* and *Malory Towers*. For younger children, she wrote *Noddy*, *The Wishing Chair* and *The Magic Faraway Tree*, among others. She died on 28 November 1968.

> **IMPORTANT FACT**
> Enid Blyton was fourteen when she won a children's poetry competition. This encouraged her to submit articles, stories and poems to magazines.

79. J.K. ROWLING

Joanne Kathleen Rowling shot to fame for creating the famous Harry Potter series. She was born on 31 July 1965. She went to Exeter University, after which she worked as a secretary and teacher, but then went through some tough times. She was unemployed for a short period of time, during which she lived in poverty.

She wrote the first Harry Potter book, *Harry Potter and the Philosopher's Stone,* in 1997. The idea for the book came to her while on a train ride. She said that she really liked the idea of creating a place where a child could have power, like Hogwarts.

Even though about 50 publishers turned her down, she never gave up. Bloomsbury Publishing bought *Harry Potter and the Philosopher's Stone* in 1997 and it was an instant success. She eventually wrote seven books in the Harry Potter series, which were so successful that they were adapted into films.

IMPORTANT FACT

J. K. Rowling published her first novel for adults, *The Casual Vacancy* in 2012. She also wrote a crime novel, *The Cuckoo's Calling* in 2013, which she says is the first of a series.

Mesmerising Musicians

This section focuses on people who have made significant contributions in the field of music. Let's find out about their talents and contributions as well as about their lives. Let's see how their music has influenced people all over the world. Read on and get to know more about these mesmerising musicians.

80. BEETHOVEN

Ludwig van Beethoven was one of the world's greatest music composers. He was born in Bonn, Germany in 1770. He wrote many symphonies, tones and pieces for music, using instruments such as the piano, organ and violin. He learned all these instruments by the young age of eight and wrote his first composition when he was only 11. He had a hearing problem which kept getting worse as he aged. Amazingly, he composed his most significant work when he was completely deaf! He died on 26 March 1827 at Vienna, Austria.

IMPORTANT FACT

Although we celebrate 17 December as his birthday, it was actually the day of his baptism. There's no accurate parish record for his birth. He is believed to have been born the day before his baptism, although it may have been a few days before. Nobody knows for sure.

81. MILES DEWEY DAVIS

Miles Dewey Davis was not only a famous American jazz musician, but also one of the most influential musicians of the 20th century. He was born in Illinois, USA, on 26 May 1926. He was only 16 when he started his career. He has led several major developments in music, including bebop, cool jazz, hard bop, modal jazz and jazz fusion. His record debut came in 1946.

IMPORTANT FACT

Nine-time Grammy Award winner Miles Davis was a major force in the jazz world, both as a trumpet player as well as a bandleader.

82. ELVIS PRESLEY

Known as the King of Rock and Roll, Elvis Presley was born on 8 January 1935 in Mississippi, USA. He came from very humble beginnings and grew to become the biggest music icon of his time. He appeared in thirty-three successful films, several television appearances and found great acclaim through his record-breaking live concerts. He is one of the highest-selling musicians of all time and has won gold, platinum and multi-platinum awards. Also under his belt are three Grammy Awards and the Grammy Lifetime Achievement Award, which he won at the age of 36. He died on 16 August 1977.

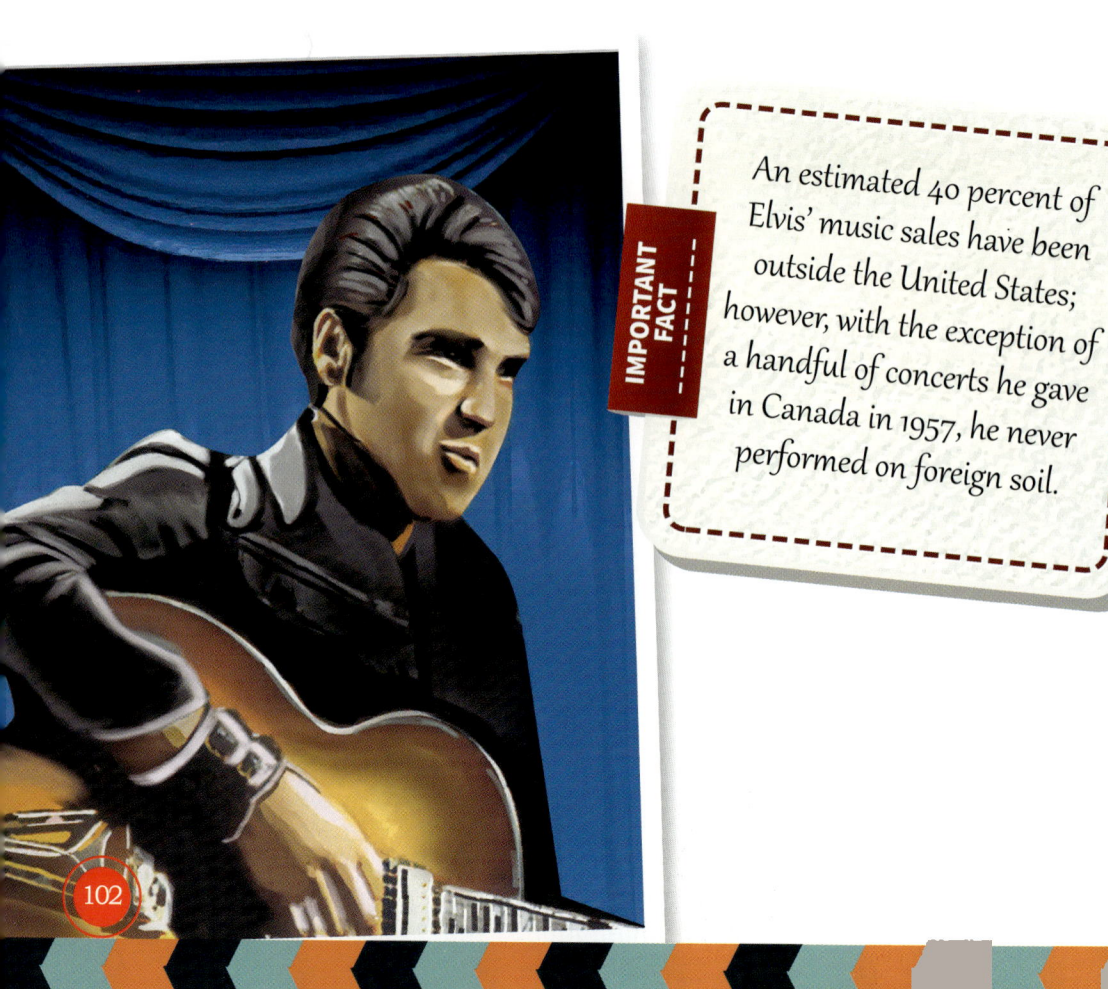

IMPORTANT FACT

An estimated 40 percent of Elvis' music sales have been outside the United States; however, with the exception of a handful of concerts he gave in Canada in 1957, he never performed on foreign soil.

83. JOHN LENNON

John Lennon was the lead singer, guitarist and song writer of the iconic musical group, 'The Beatles'. He was born on 9 October 1940 in Liverpool, England. He met Paul McCartney in 1957 and invited him to join his music group. They eventually formed the most successful songwriting partnership in musical history. Lennon left The Beatles in 1969 and later released albums with his wife, Yoko Ono. He was heavily involved with social activism which reflected in his music. A mentally unstable fan assassinated Lennon on 8 December 1980 in New York, USA.

IMPORTANT FACT

John Lennon, the great rock 'n roll rebel and iconoclast, started his singing career as a choir boy at St. Peter's church and was a member of the 3rd Allerton Boy Scout troop.

84. BOB DYLAN

Bob Dylan is an American musician, singer-songwriter, artist and writer. He was born as Robert Allen Zimmerman on 24 May 1941. He adopted the name 'Bob Dylan' while he performed folk and country songs as a college student. His thought-provoking lyrics filled with social, political and literary undertones led people to refer to him as the Shakespeare of his generation. His most famous work dates back to the 1960s, but he has remained an influential figure in pop music. He released his latest album in 2012 and continues to tour all around the world.

IMPORTANT FACT

The Nobel Prize in Literature 2016 was awarded to Bob Dylan 'for having created new poetic expressions within the great American song tradition'.

85. BOB MARLEY

Bob Marley has gone down in history for bringing Jamaican reggae music to international ears. He was born in Nine Mile, Saint Ann, Jamaica on 6 February 1945. It all started in 1963, when Marley and his friends formed a band called 'The Wailers'. Through the course of his career, Marley went on to sell more than 20 million records. He was the first superstar to emerge from a so-called backward country. Marley inspired people not just with his music, but also with his Rastafarian beliefs. He died in Miami, Florida on 11 May 1981.

86. DAVID BOWIE

In the 1970s, when he was at his peak, David Bowie was known as the master of reinvention because of his ever-changing music and appearance. He was born David Robert Jones in Brixton, South London, England on 8 January 1947. He joined six different musical groups, but none of them did well. His love for theatricals and his eccentric personality helped him soar to superstardom. He was inducted into the Rock and Roll Hall of Fame in 1996. He last released an album in 2013 after a 10-year hiatus.

> **IMPORTANT FACT**
> Bowie's first hit in the UK - Space Oddity - was used by the BBC in its coverage of the moon landing in 1969.

87. MADONNA

Madonna is often referred to as the 'Queen of Pop'. Born on 16 August 1958 in Michigan, USA, she moved to New York City to become a dancer. But fate had different plans for her. She got signed on by Sire Records and released her first music album at the age of twenty four. She continued to rule the pop music scene throughout the 1990s and 2000s. Many of her hits topped the charts at No. 1. Some of these are *Papa Don't Preach*, *Like a Prayer*, *Frozen* and *4 Minutes*.

Madonna is known to constantly reinvent herself and pleasantly surprise her audience. She has dabbled in dancing, acting, dancing and writing. Madonna even started her own entertainment company 'Maverick Entertainment'. She was inducted into the Rock and Roll Hall of Fame in 2008. In that same year, she was ranked second on the Billboard Hot 100 All-Time Top Artists. In 2013, Forbes magazine named her the fifth most powerful celebrity and also the highest-earning one.

IMPORTANT FACT

Madonna wrote a children's book *The English Roses*. Not only did it top the New York Times Best Seller list, but it also became the fastest-selling children's picture book of all time!

88. MICHAEL JACKSON

Michael Joseph Jackson—an American singer, songwriter, dancer and philanthropist, is the 'King of Pop'. He was born on 29 August 1958 in Gary, Indiana. He began his career with four of his brothers, forming the famous band, the 'Jackson 5'.

In 1968, when Jackson was only ten, Motown records signed the Jackson 5. They toured internationally, releasing six more albums between 1976 and 1984. After their success, Jackson decided to become a solo act. His debut album was *Got to be there*, which was released on 24 January 1972.

Jackson has been inducted into the Rock and Roll Hall of Fame twice. He has eight Guinness World Records throughout his successful musical career. He passed away on 25 June 2009.

IMPORTANT FACT

Michael Jackson is the highest-earning deceased artist. He has been recognised by the Guinness Book Of World Records in a new category for Highest-Earning Deceased Artist, gaining the top honour. In the first year after his passing in 2009, Jackson's estate raked in a reported $1 billion.

89. THE BEATLES

In the 1960s, a band from Liverpool, England, burst into the pop music scene and changed it forever. 'The Beatles' comprised George Harrison, John Lennon, Paul McCartney and Ringo Starr. Paul McCartney and John Lennon formed the nucleus of the group.

All the members of the band were united by a mutual love and respect for American rock and roll. They did several small-time gigs in Liverpool and Hamburg before they were spotted by Brian Epstein, a local record store owner. He was convinced of their commercial potential and became their manager. He finally got them a contract with Parlophone, a subsidiary of the giant EMI label. The Beatles soon shot to fame in the UK as well as internationally.

The Beatles were also the leaders of the counterculture that swept the world in the 1960s. Their songs were known for their anti-war, anti-capitalist stance. They were openly against the Vietnam War and John Lennon was nearly deported because of it.

IMPORTANT FACT

The Beatles remain one of the best-selling musical groups of all time. They contributed not only to music, but also to film, literature, art and fashion.

90. ABBA

ABBA was a Swedish pop group formed in Stockholm in 1972. The name was coined with the first letters of the members' names—Agnetha Fältskog, Björn Ulvaeus, Benny Andersson and Anni-Frid Lyngstad. They became the first musicians from mainland Europe to break into the British, American and Australian pop charts. ABBA put Sweden on the global music map and helped pave the way for other European musicians.

They topped the worldwide music charts throughout the 1970s. In 1974, they represented Sweden at the Eurovision Song Contest and won Sweden its first ever victory in the contest. On the contest's 50th anniversary in 2005, ABBA was felicitated again. Their song *Waterloo* was chosen as the best song in the history of the Eurovision contest. ABBA's worldwide sales were about 300–400 million. This makes them one of the highest-selling bands of all time, second only to The Beatles.

IMPORTANT FACT

In 2008, the musical Mamma Mia! was adapted into a film starring Meryl Streep. It went on to become the most successful film in the UK for that year.

Phenomenal Philosophers

This section focuses on people who have influenced the world with their ideas and ways of thinking. Some of these philosophers were well ahead of their times. They wanted to make the world a better place by influencing the minds of fellow humans. Read on and learn about the ideas, ideals and personal lives of these phenomenal philosophers.

91. SOCRATES

Socrates was a Greek philosopher whose thoughts and ideas have greatly influenced modern philosophy. He was born in Athens in 469 BCE. Although Socrates did not write any books himself, we know of his philosophies through the writings of his contemporaries and students like Plato, Aristotle and Aristophanes.

Socrates became famous because he went around Athens asking questions like 'What is beauty?', 'What is wisdom?' and 'What is the right thing to do?' He was the first to question the purpose of life.

His questions made him a controversial figure and the comic dramatists of Athens often mocked him and his beliefs. He was sentenced to death for corrupting the youth of Athens in 399 BCE.

92. ARISTOTLE

Aristotle, an ancient Greek philosopher and scientist, is considered to be one of the greatest intellectual figures of western history. He was born in 384 BCE in Greece. He is considered to have laid the foundation for Christian and Islamic philosophy. Aristotle's theories and philosophies remained pertinent even after the Renaissance. Aristotle studied under Plato at the 'Academy' for 20 years. He wrote most of his theories in the form of dialogue. He wrote extensively during this period. Plato's influence on him is evident in his writings.

Aristotle believed that the dead are more blessed and happier than the living and to die is to return to one's own home. Aristotle's intellectual range was vast. He covered many sciences as well as arts. He wrote about biology, botany, chemistry, ethics, history, logic, metaphysics, rhetoric, philosophy of mind, philosophy of science, physics, poetics, political theory, psychology and zoology. He died in 322 BCE.

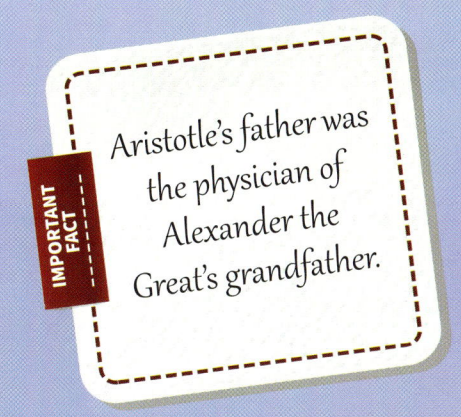

IMPORTANT FACT
Aristotle's father was the physician of Alexander the Great's grandfather.

93. PLATO

Plato was a Greek mathematician and philosopher, who is believed to be the founder of modern science and philosophy. He was born around 428 BCE in Athens. Plato is believed to have been born in a wealthy family and educated in grammar and music. He was also a student of the great philosopher Socrates. Plato founded the 'Academy', which is believed to be the first university or institute for higher learning in the world. Aristotle, one of the most famous philosophers of all time, was one of the students at the Academy.

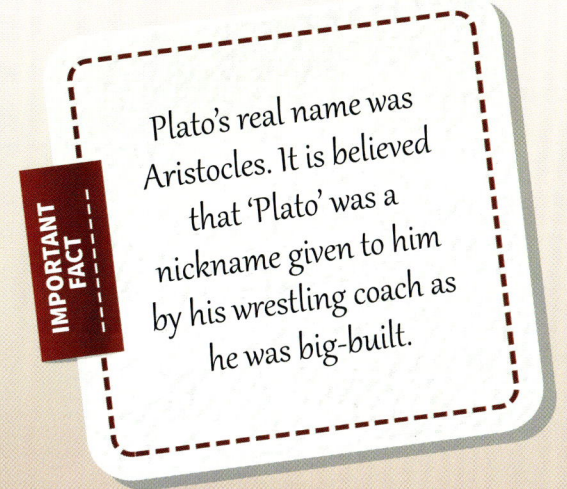

Plato believed that everything happens for a reason. He believed that the perfect models of all things on the Earth existed in a world unseen by humans. He also believed that society would remain stable and fair only if philosophers were in power. He wrote down his teachings in different forms of conversations called 'Dialogues'.

Plato's work explored justice, beauty, society and equality. He questioned aesthetics, political philosophy, theology, cosmology, language and the philosophy of life itself. He died in 347 BCE.

> **IMPORTANT FACT**
> Plato's real name was Aristocles. It is believed that 'Plato' was a nickname given to him by his wrestling coach as he was big-built.

94. SIGMUND FREUD

Sigmund Freud was an Austrian neurologist, who is known as the founder of psychoanalysis. He was born on 6 May 1856. Freud was interested in literature and was well-versed in languages like Hebrew, Latin, Spanish, German, Italian and Greek. His understanding of the human personality was very different from earlier philosophers. Freud is regarded as one of the most controversial and influential minds of all times. Freud's theory of psychoanalysis was based on resolving unconscious conflict through techniques like free association, dreams and fantasies. Freud's theories on the ego, the Oedipus and the Electra complex are some of his most influential theories. He influenced many other prominent psychologists like Erik Erikson, Alfred Alder, Carl Jung and also his own daughter, Anna Freud.

Although Freud's theories have been differently perceived by others, they have influenced and changed the field of psychology. He believed that all mental illnesses do not have physiological causes and was of the belief that cultural differences impact psychology and behaviour.

IMPORTANT FACT

Sigmund Freud published his book, *The Interpretations of Dreams*, in 1899, which laid the foundation for the theories and ideas that helped him develop his psychoanalytic theory.

95. NOAM CHOMSKY

Noam Chomsky is an American linguist, philosopher and activist, who is famous for his contributions in the field of language and mind. He was born on 7 December 1928 in Philadelphia, USA. He earned a PhD in linguistics at the University of Pennsylvania. Chomsky has been a professor for the Departments of Linguistics and Philosophy at MIT since 1955. His research has had huge ramifications for modern philosophers and psychologists, both raising and answering questions about human nature and how we process information.

Sports Stars

This section focuses on people who are remarkable sports persons. Their work has brought glory to games and inspired many people who have watched them play. Let's find out about their skills and techniques as well as their lives. Read on and get to know these sport stars.

96. MUHAMMAD ALI

Muhammad Ali, a former American professional boxer, was the first boxing champion to win the world heavyweight championship thrice. He was born on 17 January 1942 in Louisville, Kentucky, USA. He took up boxing when he was twelve. Out of the 108 amateur games he played, he won 100. He became an Olympic gold medalist in 1960. His biography is called *GOAT—A Tribute to Muhammad Ali.* GOAT is an acronym for 'Greatest Of All Time'. The book weighs 34 kg and is covered in silk and Louis Vuitton leather. The first 1,000 books were sold at USD 7,500 each.

97. STEFFI GRAF

Steffi Graf, a former German tennis player, is famous as the only tennis player to win all Grand Slam singles championships and an Olympic gold medal in the same calendar year, which was called the Golden Slam. She was born on 14 June 1969 in West Germany. Graf was coached in tennis by her father from the age of three. She dominated world tennis for over a decade in the late 1980s and 1990s. Graff ranked World No.1 for a record 377 weeks, more than any other player, male or female. She married fellow tennis star Andre Agassi in 2001. She retired in 2009.

98. RONALDO

Ronaldo Luis Nazario de Lima, a former Brazilian footballer, is one of the three players in football history to be named the World Player of the Year thrice. He was born on 18 September 1976 in Itaguai, Brazil. Ronaldo started playing football when he was twelve. He won the Golden Shoe Award in the 2002 World Cup as the highest goal scorer and helped Brazil lift the World Cup. Ronaldo's 15th goal in the 2006 World Cup made him the highest goal scorer in World Cup history. He retired from football in 2011.

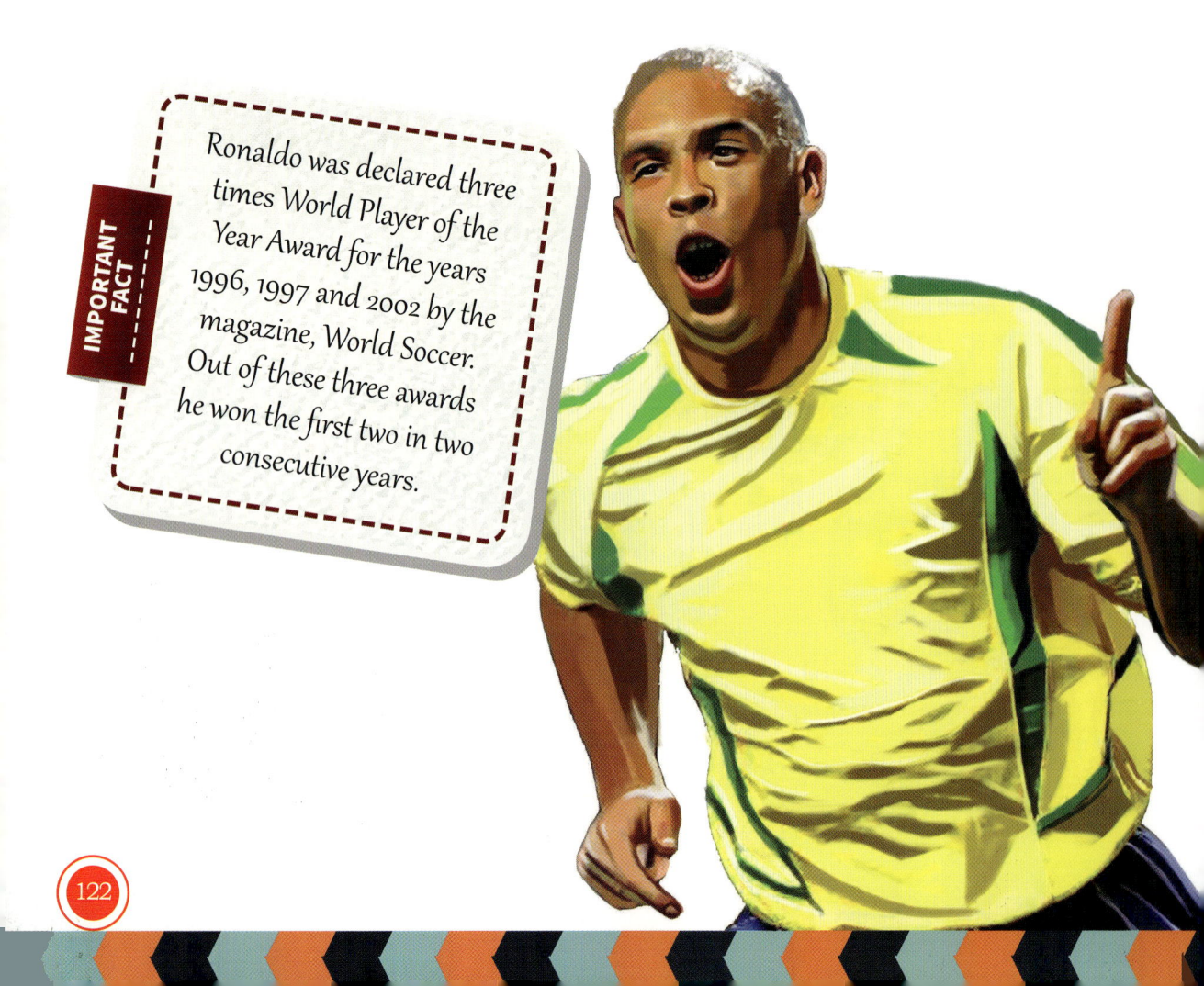

IMPORTANT FACT

Ronaldo was declared three times World Player of the Year Award for the years 1996, 1997 and 2002 by the magazine, World Soccer. Out of these three awards he won the first two in two consecutive years.

99. ROGER FEDERER

Rog0er Federer, a Swiss tennis player, is famous as the only player in the history of tennis to win 17 career men's single Grand Slam championships. He was born on 8 August 1981 in Basel, Switzerland. Federer played badminton and basketball as a child to improve his hand-eye coordination. Federer began playing tennis when he was eight. He started playing professional tennis at age 17. Federer is the only player in history to have won the Wimbledon and the US Open consecutively for three years.

IMPORTANT FACT

In 2007, Roger Federer became the first living Swiss person to be featured on a Swiss stamp. The postage picture features Roger holding the Wimbledon trophy.

100. THE WILLIAMS SISTERS

The Williams sisters are two American tennis players, Venus and Serena Williams, both of whom have been ranked as World No. 1 by the Women's Tennis Association. Venus Williams was born on 17 June 1980 in California, USA, whereas Serena Williams was born on 26 September 1981. They were both coached by their father and learnt to play tennis at a very young age. Serena and Venus Williams turned professional when they were fifteen years old.

Serena and Venus Williams won gold medals at the Sydney Olympics in 2000 and the Beijing Olympics in 2008. In 1997, Venus Williams became the first unseeded tennis player to reach the finals of the US Open. Serena defeated Venus in the finals of the French Open, US Open and Wimbledon to win all three tournaments in 2002. Venus Williams has won seven Grand Slam titles and Serena Williams has won 17 Grand Slam titles.

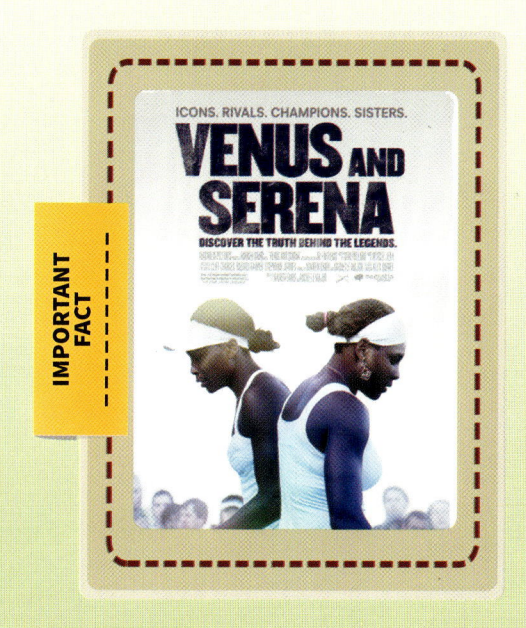

THE 2013 FILM VENUS AND SERENA CAPTURES WILLIAM SISTERS' LIFE ON CELLULOID

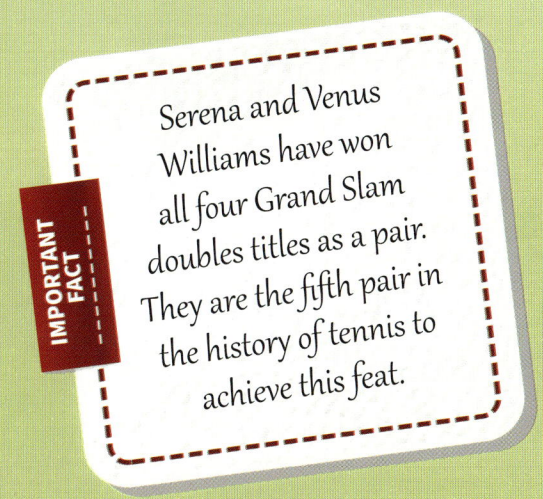

IMPORTANT FACT

Serena and Venus Williams have won all four Grand Slam doubles titles as a pair. They are the fifth pair in the history of tennis to achieve this feat.

101. USAIN BOLT

IMPORTANT FACT

Bolt published a memoir, *My Story: 9:58: The World's Fastest Man*, in 2010. It was expanded and reissued as *The Fastest Man Alive: The True Story of Usain Bolt* in 2012.

Usain Bolt, a Jamaican sprinter, is the first athlete to win six Olympic gold medals in sprinting. He was born on 21 August 1986 in Trelawny, Jamaica. Bolt was interested in cricket and football when he was young. In fact, he was an outstanding fast bowler. But he was guided towards track and field by his coaches. Bolt won a gold medal for track and field racing when he was fifteen years old. This made him the youngest person to ever win a world championship in any event.

By the time he was 17, he broke the junior world record for the 200 m run. He was also the first teenager to run it in less than 20 seconds.

In the 2008 Olympics, Bolt became the second athlete after Carl Lewis to win the 100 m, 200 m and the 4 x 100 m relay, and set world records in all three races. Bolt is believed to be the fastest man alive.

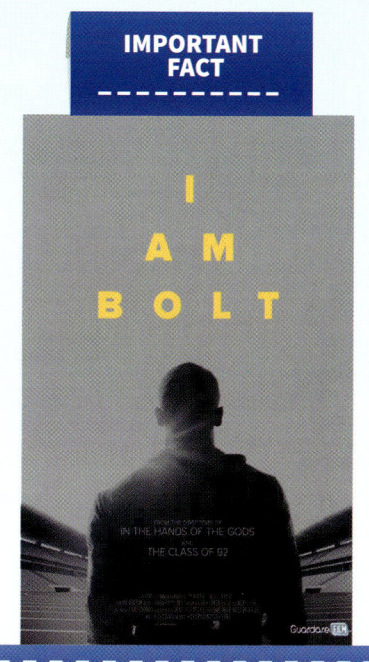

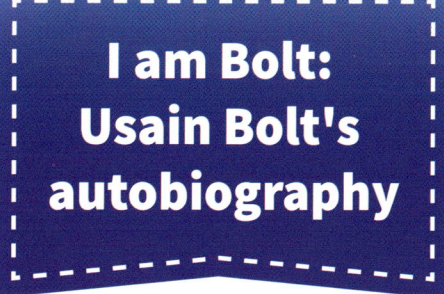

IMPORTANT FACT

I am Bolt: Usain Bolt's autobiography

OTHER TITLES IN THIS SERIES

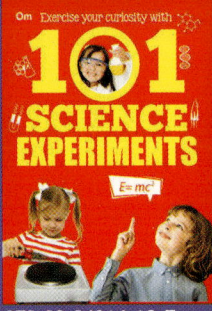

- 101 Science Experiments — 978-93-86316-12-7 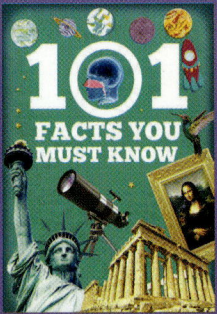
- 101 Facts You Must Know — 978-93-86316-08-0 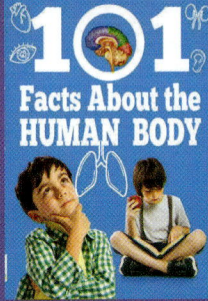
- 101 Facts About the Human Body — 978-93-86316-09-7 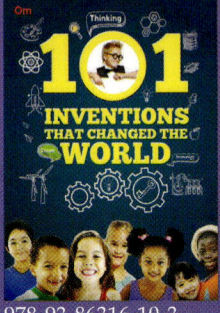
- 101 Inventions That Changed the World — 978-93-86316-10-3 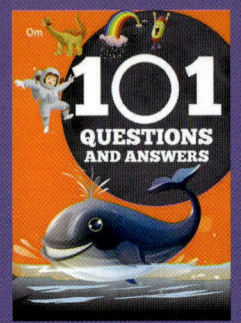
- 101 Questions and Answers — 978-93-81607-39-8 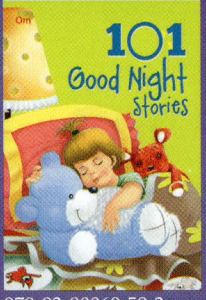
- 101 Good Night Stories — 978-93-80069-59-3 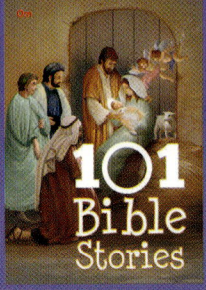
- 101 Bible Stories — 978-93-80069-87-6 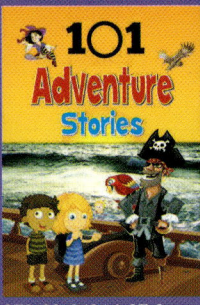
- 101 Adventure Stories — 978-93-86316-07-3 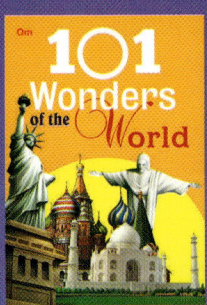
- 101 Wonders of the World — 978-93-80070-78-0 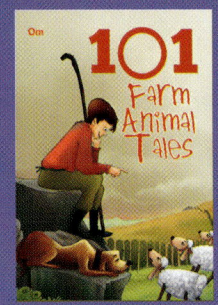
- 101 Farm Animal Tales — 978-93-80069-85-2 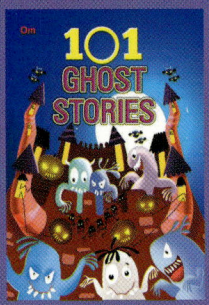
- 101 Ghost Stories — 978-93-80069-90-6 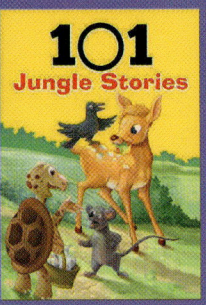
- 101 Jungle Stories — 978-93-80069-57-9 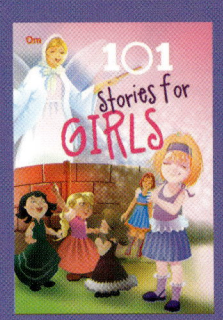
- 101 Stories for Girls — 978-93-80070-76-6 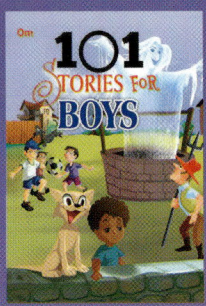
- 101 Stories for Boys — 978-93-80070-75-9 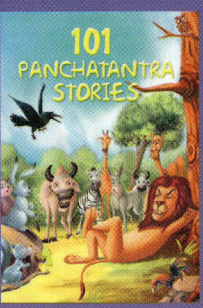
- 101 Panchatantra Stories — 978-93-80070-77-3 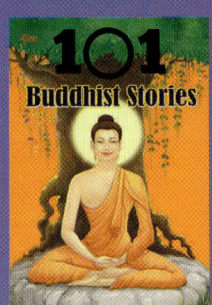
- 101 Buddhist Stories — 978-93-80069-58-6 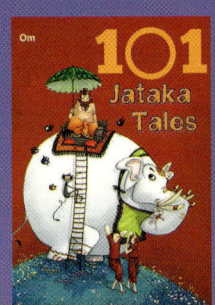
- 101 Jataka Tales — 978-93-81607-35-0

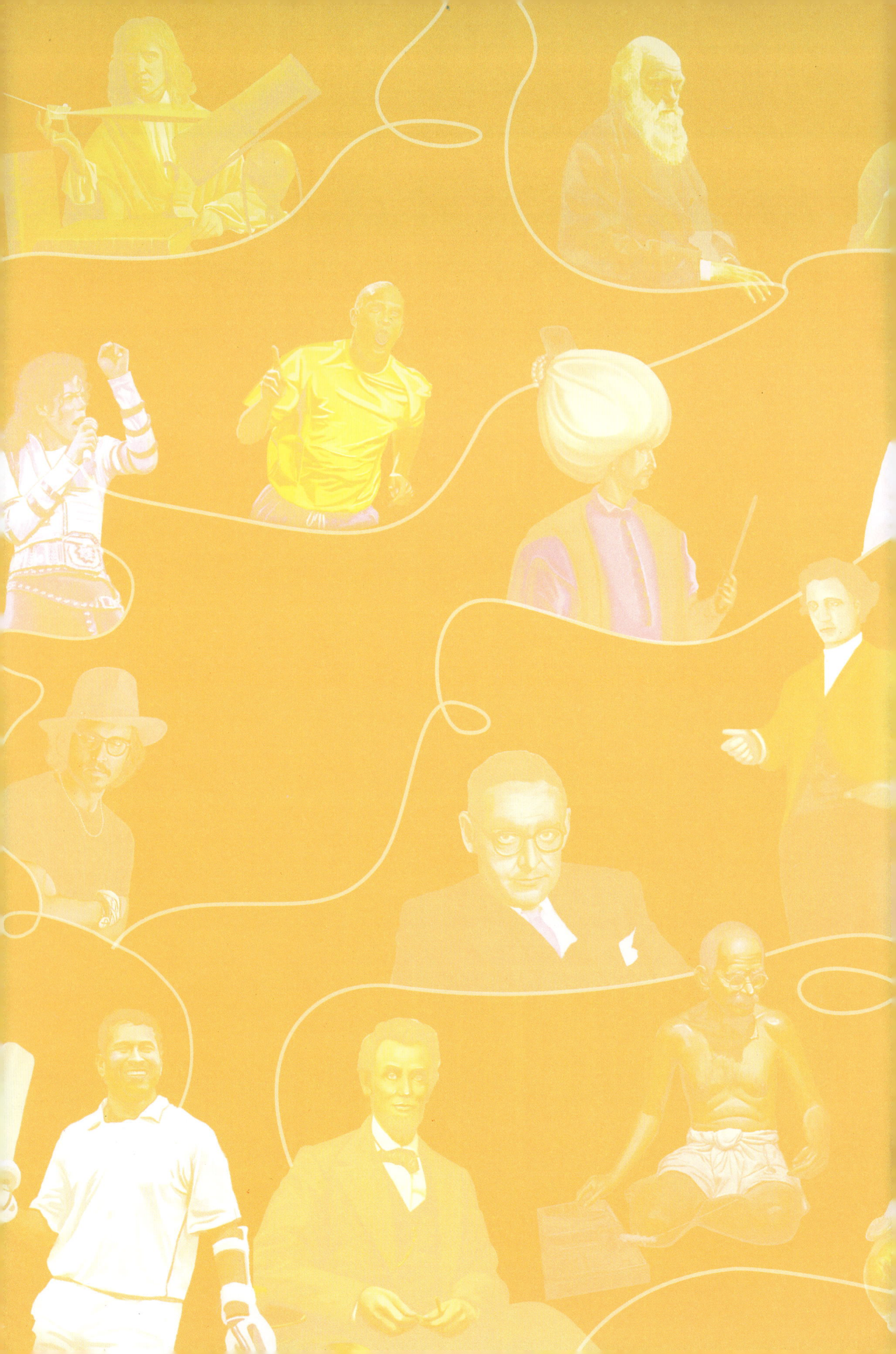